**Disturbing Development in the Jim Crow South**

**GEOGRAPHIES OF JUSTICE AND SOCIAL TRANSFORMATION**

SERIES EDITORS

Mathew Coleman, *Ohio State University*
Sapana Doshi, *University of California, Merced*

FOUNDING EDITOR

Nik Heynen, *University of Georgia*

ADVISORY BOARD

Deborah Cowen, *University of Toronto*
Zeynep Gambetti, *Boğaziçi University*
Geoff Mann, *Simon Fraser University*
James McCarthy, *Clark University*
Beverley Mullings, *Queen's University*
Harvey Neo, *Singapore University of Technology and Design*
Geraldine Pratt, *University of British Columbia*
Ananya Roy, *University of California, Los Angeles*
Michael Watts, *University of California, Berkeley*
Ruth Wilson Gilmore, *CUNY Graduate Center*
Jamie Winders, *Syracuse University*
Melissa W. Wright, *Pennsylvania State University*
Brenda S. A. Yeoh, *National University of Singapore*

# Disturbing Development in the Jim Crow South

**MONA DOMOSH**

THE UNIVERSITY OF GEORGIA PRESS
*Athens*

Published by the University of Georgia Press
Athens, Georgia 30602
www.ugapress.org
© 2023 by Mona Domosh
All rights reserved
Designed by
Set in 10.25/13.5 Minion 3 Regular by Copperline Book Services.

Most University of Georgia Press titles are available
from popular e-book vendors.

Printed digitally

Library of Congress Cataloging-in-Publication Data
Names: Domosh, Mona, 1957- author.
Title: Disturbing development in the Jim Crow South / Mona Domosh.
Description: Athens : The University of Georgia Press, [2023] | Series: Geographies of justice and social transformation | Includes bibliographical references and index.
Identifiers: LCCN 2022034720 | ISBN 9780820363417 (hardback) | ISBN 9780820363424 (paperback) | ISBN 9780820363431 (epub) | ISBN 9780820363554 (pdf)
Subjects: LCSH: Daly, Laura Randolph. | United States. Department of Agriculture—Officials and employees—Biography. | African American farmers—Southern States—Economic conditions—20th century. | African American farmers—Southern States—Social conditions—20th century. | Southern States—Race relations—History—20th century. | Southern States—Economic conditions—1918-
Classification: LCC HD1773.A5 D65 2023 | DDC 338.10975—dc23/eng/20220907
LC record available at https://lccn.loc.gov/2022034720

# CONTENTS

List of Figures  vii

Acknowledgments  ix

**CHAPTER 1**  Laura R. Daly and the United States Department of Agriculture  1

**CHAPTER 2**  Home Demonstration Work and the Sustaining of Black Life  21

**CHAPTER 3**  The Movable School and the Aesthetics of Uplift  44

**CHAPTER 4**  Prairie Farms and the Struggle for Black Land Ownership  69

**CHAPTER 5**  Black Extension Work in the U.S. South and Liberal Development Overseas  95

Conclusion  117

Notes  127

Index  153

# FIGURES

| | | |
|---|---|---|
| 1.1 | Map of Montgomery County | 2 |
| 1.2 | Laura R. Daly demonstrating canning techniques | 3 |
| 2.1 | Women and girls of the Mabelvale Home Demonstration Club | 27 |
| 2.2 | Laura R. Daly demonstrating canning techniques | 30 |
| 2.3 | Women with their babies watching a demonstrator weigh an infant | 32 |
| 2.4 | Women sit on the porch of a new home | 32 |
| 2.5 | Women, children, and a man posed outside of a home | 33 |
| 2.6 | Women and children chat on the front porch | 33 |
| 2.7 | Laura R. Daly talks with a family on their porch | 34 |
| 2.8 | Mrs. Jamerson posed in front of a display of canned goods | 43 |
| 3.1 | The movable school in 1917 | 48 |
| 3.2 | Before the movable school came | 51 |
| 3.3 | After the movable school came | 51 |
| 3.4 | Woman weaving a basket and children posed in front of a house | 60 |
| 3.5 | Before and after photographs of an improved outdoor toilet | 61 |
| 3.6 | Before and after photographs of Hill Taylor's farm | 63 |
| 3.7 | Tom Moss's old and new home | 64 |
| 4.1 | Farm family posed outside their new home | 70 |
| 4.2 | Mrs. Brown displaying her canned goods in the smokehouse | 70 |
| 4.3 | Prairie Farms cooperative store | 71 |
| 4.4 | Prairie Farms community building and school | 71 |
| 4.5 | Perspective and plan for Prairie Farms two-bedroom farmhouse | 78 |
| 4.6 | Perspective and plan for Prairie Farms three-bedroom farmhouse | 78 |

| | | |
|---|---|---|
| 4.7 | Remnants of farming area near Tuskegee | 81 |
| 4.8 | Small home with a woman and child hanging laundry outside | 81 |
| 4.9 | Woman with children posed outside a farmhouse | 82 |
| 4.10 | Family posed outside their small farm home | 82 |
| 4.11 | Man with children posed on a wagon with oxen | 84 |
| 4.12 | Classroom in the Prairie Farms school | 84 |
| 4.13 | Fred Smith's old home | 92 |
| 4.14 | Fred Smith's new home under construction | 92 |
| 5.1 | The East African Educational Commission | 101 |
| 5.2 | Thomas Campbell surrounded by children | 104 |
| 5.3 | Thomas Campbell with unidentified group in Africa | 104 |
| 5.4 | Thomas Campbell and Claude Wickard with map of Africa | 108 |
| 5.5 | Thomas Campbell and Claude Wickard with globe | 108 |
| 5.6 | Women in India watching an infant being weighed | 114 |
| C.1 | Laura R. Daly as field representative | 118 |

## ACKNOWLEDGMENTS

This book begins and ends with Laura Blanche Randolph Daly, a person that I know only through the writings she left behind and from the memories of Barbara Jean Morgan Lawler, whose godmother Mildred Daly Maxwell was Laura Daly's daughter. On the pages in between I've done my best to absorb those writings and memories and use them as a guide for understanding and explaining Daly's (and by extension her colleagues') work with the USDA (United States Department of Agriculture) at Tuskegee and appreciating the achievements of the Black cooperative extension service. She has served as an inspiration for the book and my personal connection to a time and place very different from my own, although I too once called Montgomery, Alabama, home. In working on this project I have been mindful of my own positionality, especially my whiteness, which has shaped my understanding and at times circumscribed my explanations. I am incredibly grateful to the many Black scholars in geography, history, and related fields whose insights and interventions have helped me see and interpret Daly's and her colleagues' work and achievements. Thank you, Barbara Lawler, for welcoming me to your house and sharing with me your memories and photographs of Laura R. Daly. An acknowledgement seems too weak a gesture for what I owe Daly and all of her colleagues that I write about here. I hope this book provides a first step toward honoring their accomplishments.

I was only able to understand those accomplishments because of reviewers, editors, and interlocuters who offered a series of critical interventions that helped me realize the limitations of my original narrative. I am forever indebted to them for taking the time to correct what I had wrong, to challenge my racist intellectual frameworks, and to redirect my vision so that I could see what had been in front of me all along. Thank you to the amazing anonymous reviewers of this book manuscript, to the anonymous reviewers of the three previously published articles I wrote based on this work, to the editors who shepherded this work through to publication (Katherine McKittrick, Nik Heynen, Simon Naylor), and to the many interlocuters who listened to presentations I gave and provided essential critical feedback. I owe a huge debt to Rod Neumann who agreed to read a version of this manuscript and provide feedback when it was sorely needed. Robert Zababwa at Tuskegee University read chapter 4 and pointed out critical errors in my narrative. He also took me on a tour of Prairie Farms and shared with me his wealth of knowledge about its history and current status. I am forever grateful. My engagement with the field of Black Geographies has been fundamental to the framing of this book. Thank you to the many scholars who have devoted their time and energy to establishing this important intellectual agenda that has provided new frameworks for understanding the world

I am extremely fortunate to have colleagues at the Department of Geography at Dartmouth whom I learn from every day. I am particularly grateful to those who have inspired me through their own work to challenge the norms of historical geography and human geography more broadly—Treva Ellison, Susanne Freidberg, Patricia Lopez, Abby Neely, and Darius Scott. Thank you to the co-organizers—Brian S. Williams and Yui Hashimoto—and the other participants of our departmental racial capitalism reading group. My engagements with postdoctoral fellows in the Geography Department and the Society of Fellows have been some of the most fruitful and enjoyable of my career. Many of my initial speculations about how and why the Black cooperative extension service of the USDA was interesting and important came about in conversations with Kevin Grove, Paul Jackson, and Kate Hall, while later conversations happened over seminar tables and dinner drinks with postdocs in the Society of Fellows.

This research could never have been completed without the assistance provided by archivists and librarians at a range of institutions: Auburn University, Tuskegee University, Mississippi State University, University of Arkansas, the National Archives, the Alabama Department of Archives and History, Burke Library at Union Theological Seminary, the School of Oriental and African Studies at the University of London, the Schomburg Center for Research in Black Culture, the Pitt Rivers Museum, and the Rockefeller Archive Center. Thank you to the staff of these institutions for graciously and generously devoting their time to helping me track down documents and record the information that I needed. Dana Chandler at Tuskegee University Archives welcomed me to town by taking me to a local meat-and-three restaurant for lunch. His interest in and support for my work never waned. Thank you, Dana, and the staff, at the Tuskegee University Archives, particularly Cheryl Ferguson who found documents for me that had gone missing. At Auburn University Libraries Special Collections and Archives, I am grateful to John Varner and Dwayne Cox. Sorting through all the material and putting the pieces together into a coherent frame was a daunting task. Some terrific Dartmouth Geography undergraduate students helped me as research assistants: Anna Driscoll, Emma Esterman, Rachel Funk, Nathan Greenstein, Amenah Hasan, Britta McComber, Victoria McCraven, and Anna Staropoli. I was lucky to have the dream team of Katelyn Walker and Emily Weiswasser working with me at the initial stages of this project. It was a joy and an honor to think with them.

Mat Coleman and Sapana Doshi, the editors of the Geographies of Justice and Social Transformation series at the University of Georgia Press, welcomed this book to their series and maintained their support through several bumps in the road. Thank you for believing in this manuscript and rooting for its publication. It has been a pleasure to work with Mick Gusinde-Duffy at the University of Georgia Press. He has patiently guided this manuscript through several revisions, given equal weight to criticisms and praise, and kept the process moving forward toward publication. Thank you. It is important to me that this book looks and feels a particular way since I want to give voice and visibility to people who have been hidden from most histories, and so I am incredibly grateful to the production and design team at the University of Georgia Press, particularly Jon Davies, and Lisa Stallings at Longleaf Services.

Portions of chapter 1 were originally published in the *Annals of the American Association of Geographers* as "Genealogies of Race, Gender, and Place," 2017, vol. 107, no. 3, pp. 765–778, and I want to thank the publisher Taylor and Francis for granting permission to use that text. Some of the text in chapter 2 appeared in "Practising Development at Home: Race, Gender, and the 'Development' of the American South," *Antipode*, vol. 47, 4, 2015, pp. 915–941; while portions of chapter 5 were originally published in "Race, Biopolitics, and Liberal Development from the Jim Crow South to Postwar Africa," *Transactions of the Institute of British Geographers*, vol. 43, 2018, pp. 312–324. Thank you to Tuskegee University Archives, Special Collections at the University of Arkansas Libraries, and Auburn University Libraries Special Collections and Archives for allowing me to use some of their images in this book. I am grateful to Dartmouth College for granting me a Senior Faculty Fellowship that provided the time I needed to complete my original manuscript, and to the National Science Foundation (#1262774) that funded most of the research.

Any opinions, findings, and conclusions or recommendations expressed in this material are those of the author and do not necessarily reflect the views of the National Science Foundation.

The COVID-19 pandemic and its periodic lockdowns and cancellations has only made clearer what I've known for a very long time, and that is how much I rely on my friends and family to sustain me and my work. Over zoom, on the phone, through texts, or in person, they have listened to my woes, distracted me with good humor, given me cause for celebration, and reminded me what really matters in life. Thank you all. I could never have completed this book without you: Susan Ackerman, Sheila Culbert, Mary Desjardins, Amy Haff, Derek Haff, Annie Halliday, Beth Halliday, Courtney Halliday, Gail Hollander, Melissa Hyams, Brian Lundy, Katt Lundy, Nancy Lundy, Joe Lundy, Laura McDaniel, Jo Beth Mertens, Peggy Mevs, Martha Neary, Rod Neumann, Kelly Palmer, Connie Reimer, David Rubien, Joni Seager, Richard Sealey, Christopher Sneddon, Stuart Weiss, Mark Williams, Jay Wojnarowski, and Richard Wright. No one has listened to more of my woes than Frank Magilligan. At the end of a long day, it is his presence that soothes me. He has also read and edited this entire book. Thank you, Frank, for supporting me no matter what, for listening when I needed to be heard, and for (almost) always being able to make me laugh.

**Disturbing Development in
the Jim Crow South**

**CHAPTER 1**

# Laura R. Daly and the United States Department of Agriculture

Just a few years after the passage of the Smith-Lever Bill, a federal law that provided funding for the cooperative extension service of the United States Department of Agriculture (USDA) including its Home Demonstration Unit, Laura R. Daly completed her annual report by drawing a map indicating the locations, types, and numbers of home demonstration activities that she had conducted during the calendar year of 1919.[1] It constituted one part of the standard reporting forms that each USDA extension service agent had to complete yearly. This visual tool would have provided USDA local, regional, and national officials with a quick snapshot of how their cooperative extension program was being practiced on the ground. In this instance, those practices were taking place in a city—Montgomery, Alabama—somewhat surprising given the USDA's cooperative extension service's mandate of improving farming and rural life. So, too, a focus on the home instead of the fields might seem out of place for a federal agency charged with agricultural improvements. Like other home demonstrators, Laura Daly's work came packaged with a set of assumptions about the relationships between home life (both urban and rural) and rural improvement that the U.S. government found important enough to invest in. And for Daly, the role that race played in that relationship (between home life and rural improvement) was explicit and at the forefront of her work, because what the map also indicates, obvious to local officials at the time, is that Daly was Black. Her map sketches out the racial segregation patterns in Montgomery, with Black residents dominating the parts of the city where she worked, to the west of downtown, and pockets just to the east and northwest. The USDA's cooperative extension service was racially segregated, and Daly was one of the first African American women to be appointed an agent in the state of Alabama.

2   Chapter One

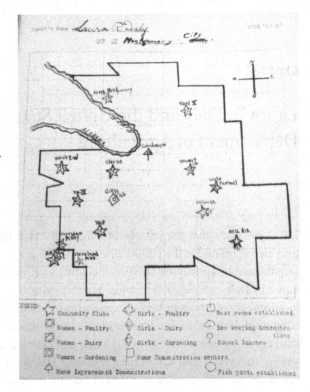

FIGURE 1.1. Map of Montgomery County, AL showing home demonstration work, drawn by Laura R. Daly. Laura R. Daly, *Annual Report of Home Demonstration Work for Women and Girls, calendar year 1919*, 1919, ACES Collection (Alabama Cooperative Extension Service), box 107. Courtesy of Auburn University Libraries Special Collections and Archives.

I open this book with a focus on Laura Daly because her work and life embodied the concessions and negotiations involved in working for the USDA as a Black woman operating within the racial and gendered socioeconomic system that characterized the Jim Crow South. As figure 1.1 indicates, Daly spent most of her working time in Montgomery during 1919 visiting women's community clubs, with the addition of one home demonstration activity and one girls' poultry club. More commonly, however, Daly worked with women living in rural areas, helping them with the home production of food and clothing (fig. 1.2) and providing instruction in home health care, similar to the work conducted by white home demonstration agents. Yet unlike those white agents, her work helping farm women was intended to produce outcomes more significant than better food and clothing. As a graduate of Hampton Institute in Virginia, an educational institution begun by white philanthropists to provide practical education for African Americans,[2] and a woman who spent most of her working life as an employee of the African American extension service based at Booker T. Washington's Tuskegee Institute, Daly's edu-

FIGURE 1.2. Photograph of Laura R. Daly demonstrating canning techniques to women. Original caption: Negro agent demonstrating canning methods, home of Frank Taylor, Montgomery, AL. ACES Collection. Courtesy of Auburn University Libraries Special Collections and Archives.

cation and work life were saturated with a set of beliefs about how to uplift her race.[3] From a close reading of her USDA annual reports (particularly the narrative sections where she was allowed to write freely), her letters that are saved at Tuskegee and Auburn universities' archives, and from meeting with a relative of hers, I concluded that Daly was a firm believer in the discourse of racial uplift and a practitioner of what Higginbotham refers to as "respectability politics."[4] She trusted that her role in Black society was to uplift less fortunate women by showing them how, through hard work and self-help, they could better themselves and gradually make it up the ladder of success. This role as an agent of uplift aligned with many of the goals of the USDA's extension service, but not with others. The improvement of rural living conditions for white farmers, in other words, did not come with the extra burden of uplifting a race. Furthermore, Daly's everyday work and life were conducted within the dictates of white supremacy that curtailed any movement toward racial parity.[5] Daly's goal of helping Black women to help themselves was attainable only up to a point; beyond teaching poor Black farmers how to care for themselves (and therefore relieving landlords of the cost of social reproduction of their laborers), the Jim Crow South had no use for Black rural improvement.

*Disturbing Development in the Jim Crow South* explores the quagmire USDA employees like Daly faced: how to practice rural improvement in ways that supported Black farmers' lives within the Jim Crow South whose form of racial capitalism—plantation agriculture—relied on the devaluing of those lives. By racial capitalism, I refer to the ways in which racism was and is a founding and constitutive structure of inequality underpinning capitalism.[6] As Melamed explains, capital accumulation requires the production of human difference: "Capital can only be capital when it is accumulating, and it can only accumulate by producing and moving through relations of severe inequality among human groups ... racism enshrines the inequalities that capitalism requires."[7] The plantation agriculture that characterized the Cotton Belt of Alabama where Laura Daly lived and worked was a form of racial capitalism, a form that relied on disposable, racialized, labor to maintain the profitability of its large-scale, export-driven agricultural product.[8] This book examines how Black USDA employees reworked federal mandates and re-imagined federal projects to disturb that system. By focusing on the practices developed by the USDA's African American extension service instead of on the policies of the U.S. federal government, this book reveals how government interventions aimed at one set of goals were subtly transformed and tweaked by Black extension service agents into serving their own goals. The intended objective of the USDA's cooperative extension service was to modernize U.S. agriculture not only through the dissemination of new agricultural knowledges and technologies but also through the dissemination of new ways of living. In other words, like many other Progressive-era reform movements, the USDA's extension service was dispensing advice on how to create "better" and more "modern" citizens. In this way, the extension service was practicing what scholars have referred to as "liberal development," that is, interventions aimed at self-improvement.[9] Thus it was not unusual for extension service employees both Black and white to work in urban and rural areas. As a Black woman working for the extension service, however, Laura Daly's job came with a set of complications that did not trouble her white counterparts, because some of the federal-level schemes to improve Black lives presented threats to the white supremacy that characterized the Jim Crow South.

## Negotiating, Transforming, Resisting Liberal Development

This book documents how Laura Daly, and the many other Black employees of the USDA's extension service, dealt with these complications. For them to succeed in supporting poor Black farmers, they had to conduct their work quietly without drawing attention from white landlords. Simultaneously, they had to legitimize their work to USDA officials by documenting their success stories. Daly and her fellow USDA agents therefore were engaged daily in a difficult and subtle balancing act: trying to support Black farmers without raising local white supremacists' ire, all the while legitimizing their work to the USDA. This book details how they accomplished this; how, in other words, they sometimes translated USDA's directives, sometimes transformed those directives, and sometimes created their own directives in order to support poor Black farmers by teaching them about food production and health care, and by promoting land and home ownership. And they did all of this rather stealthily, slowly, without drawing local attention. Daly and her fellow USDA agents, I suggest, were engaged in a quiet and subtle form of resistance, a polite politics that was specifically meant *not* to draw attention because to do so would have put an end to their work. James Scott's term "weapons of the weak" gets close to what I mean here by a quiet and subtle politics, but what I am suggesting, drawing on the works of feminist, anticolonial, and antiracist scholars, is a form of resistance that was specifically meant to go unnoticed and hence unchallenged.[10] And because Black USDA agents' actions that transformed and translated directives were subtle, their presence is not easily detected in verbal and visual material that is collected in historical archives.

Almost all of the material in the various archives that I examined in order to understand Daly and her fellow USDA agents are documents produced by or for official state bureaucracies, including the USDA's various local, regional, and federal offices and, as in chapter 4, the various offices of the Farm Security Administration. Therefore, people like Daly were not writing about how their daily actions and cumulative accomplishments were meant to eventually bring about racial and economic justice (the goal of uplift), nor did they state that they were ignoring some of the USDA's directives that made little sense to them. I only began to realize the nature of those actions and accomplishments when I paid very close attention to what was being repeated over and over in words and images, and therefore by contrast to what was barely noted. Instead of reading "against the grain" of the archive, searching for evidence of resistance, I read "along the grain" paying close attention to the "archive's granular rather than seamless texture."[11] As Ann Laura Stoler suggests, "the search for dramatic 'reversal,' 'usurpation,' and successful 'appropriation' can hide 'events' that are muted in their consequences, less bellicose in their seizures, less spectacular in how and what they reframe."[12] And certainly what Daly and her fellow Black USDA agents were enacting through their various tweakings and transformations of top-down mandates were not "reversals" of policies or "usurpations" of doctrine but instead were "events" that were muted and intentionally unnoted. What Daly and other Black USDA agents emphasized through repetition of particular phrases, stories, and images in their official documentation were accounts of racial uplift, that is, accounts that highlighted how the USDA was improving Black farmers lives. What was not mentioned in these accounts was the "bellicose" and "spectacular" political significance of the endpoint of the process of uplift, that is, racial equity. To do so would have drawn attention to the threat posed by the work of Daly and her fellow USDA agents, since racial equity undermined the devaluing of Black lives that sustained plantation agriculture.

By reading along the grain of the archives, therefore, I have been able to understand how Black USDA agents struggled to support poor Black farmers and participate in racial uplift within (not against) the framework provided by the USDA's extension service, a framework built from liberal assumptions about rural improvement. The process of racial uplift, in other words, could easily be framed as aided self-help if the implications of its endpoint—racial parity—were ignored. I use the term "liberal" to refer to development interventions aimed at self-improvement and self-sustenance; schemes, in other words, meant to help people help themselves. Mark Duffield defines liberal forms of development as those that assume "problem" populations, through self-help, can use outside aid to improve their lives and livelihoods, and suggests a long historical arc that connects contemporary liberal development practices to the origins of Western modernity itself and its imagined contrast with an inadequate "other."[13] As scholars from a range of disciplinary perspectives have shown, that arc is comprised of innumerable strands that weave in and out of one another, intersecting at particular times and places when powerful interests coalesce around shared anxieties.[14] This book examines the Cotton Belt of the Jim Crow South as one such intersection, an intersection that highlights the roots of liberal development schemes in the anti-Black racism that constituted plantation agriculture, and how these schemes, conceived in lofty government offices distant from their targeted populations, bump up against the realities of regional and local social, economic, and political systems, and can be quietly and subtly resisted. The USDA's rural improvement projects were bounded by the constraints of an economic system that favored landlords over tenants, and capital accumulation over self-sufficiency and subsistence agriculture. Thus, improvements to the living conditions of poor often landless farmers could only go so far. In the Cotton Belt of the Jim Crow South, those constraints were constituted in racial terms. It's not that all landlords were white and all tenant farmers and sharecroppers were Black; the overall numbers tell a more complicated story. In general, whites outnumbered Blacks as tenant farmers and sharecroppers in Alabama and Georgia, but in many of the counties that constituted the heart of the Cotton Belt, such as Macon County, Alabama, Black sharecroppers and tenant farmers far outnumbered white farmers.[15] It's that the profits and power garnered through cotton production were sustained through a structure of beliefs and practices that normalized the supremacy of white people over Black people. The long history of slavery and plantation geographies shaped those relations of power, profit, and race into hardened layers of sediment, forming a bulwark of institutions, practices, and beliefs that were seemingly as fixed and unmovable as granite.[16] Even the physical geography of the region became affixed to race. The use of the term "Black Belt" originally referred to the rich, dark, Vertisols of the uplands of Alabama and Georgia that attracted white settlers to the region in the 1820s and 1830s, yet it soon came to refer not only to soil but to the laborers who worked it.[17]

This case study of the USDA's African American extension service highlights, therefore, how liberal development schemes can be disrupted through collective action. The USDA's extension service's mandate was the same for its white and Black divisions; their agents used the same reporting forms and in theory conducted identical work. The differences in their practices originated not in Washington, D.C., but in Tuskegee, Alabama—home to the USDA's Black extension service for the region covering the Cotton Belt—and the people who made these decisions were not national-level, white bureaucrats, but local, African American USDA agents. And they made these decisions because, as Black people living in the heart of the Jim Crow South, they understood the limitations of federal power within the context of white supremacy. Negotiating between these various powers, agents like Daly forged a path for themselves that they believed combined the USDA's extension service goals with their own goals of racial uplift. In essence, they were using federal dollars and power to fuel their own objectives. Different actors and agencies had competing agendas: for the federal government, the agenda was to control the perceived economic and social threat posed by tenancy and sharecropping; for southern, white, landlords, it was to maintain a healthy and inexpensive labor force; and for local Black leaders, it was to gradually improve African American living conditions so as to achieve racial and economic justice.

And even though Laura Daly and her coworkers at Tuskegee had to answer to federal and regional supervisors and therefore had to accept their goals to some degree, they translated those goals into practices that suited their interest in improving Black farmers' lives. The idea of racial uplift as espoused by African American leaders like Booker T. Washington posited that through hard work and self-improvement, Blacks in the United States could gradually move their way up the hierarchy to eventual equity. W. E. B. Du Bois famously opposed this strategy, suggesting that uplift, particularly as given voice by Washington's forceful Atlanta speech of 1895, was a compromise that gave in to southern whites' demands for continued segregation and disenfranchisement as the price to be paid by southern Blacks in exchange for better living conditions and schooling. Du Bois's strategy called for political action against the institutions and practices that upheld white supremacy. Although seemingly opposing visions, recent scholarship has suggested that the differences in the two strategies in terms of defining the means—gradual progress versus direct confrontation—have been overplayed at the expense of the similarities in goals, that of racial equality.[18] Nonetheless, it was Washington's vision of gradual uplift through self-improvement that shaped the USDA's African American extension service, and thus it is Washington's vision as put into practice at Tuskegee—not Du Bois's—that forms the focus of this book. Laura Daly and her coworkers did not directly confront white supremacy, but they offered a space for helping Black rural communities improve their living conditions. And they did so by translating the biopolitical mandate of the USDA into practices that could actually support Black farmers.[19]

Thus, this book interrogates an important episode in the long history of Black agricultural resistance movements. Geographers and other scholars have documented the myriad ways that Black people have forged meaningful lives and resisted racial capitalism through working on and with the land, from the gardens created and maintained by enslaved peoples in the U.S. South, to Black agricultural cooperatives in the Jim Crow era, to the preservation of Black foodways and food provisioning, to contemporary urban farmer activists.[20] According to Monica White, what these efforts share are an insistence on collective agency and community resilience. Taken together these terms refer to the ways in which, at certain times and places, an aggrieved group of people "comes together and believes in their mutual success" and so acts in a way to support community and to "build alternatives to existing political and economic relationships." These everyday acts of resistance, she argues, are "not disruptive but rather constructive" since they concentrate on "ways to adjust, withstand, and absorb disturbances, and to reorganize while undergoing change."[21] In addition, as Bledsoe and Wright have argued, these acts of resistance share a commitment to "*not* treating the natural environment as something to be exploited for the accumulation of capital."[22] What I argue in this book is that through their various negotiations, translations, and creations, Daly and her fellow Black employees at the USDA were involved in collective activities that promoted community resilience by treating the natural environment as a source of food and sustenance, and by conceiving of land ownership as a form of economic freedom. Although they were not farming themselves, these employees based at Tuskegee were carrying forward the mission that Booker T. Washington had established in the institution's early days, a mission that looked to land ownership and Black farming as a strategy of resistance. Their efforts were constructive as they struggled to find strategies that could leverage the resources of the USDA to support the lives and livelihoods of Black farmers in the Cotton Belt of the Jim Crow South. And although the goal of land ownership was not always attained, the struggles of Daly and her fellow USDA employees as they went about their everyday practices of home and farm demonstration and as they worked to translate federal mandates were themselves constitutive of alternative geographies, that is, these everyday sociospatial acts formed what McKittrick and Woods call Black geographies: "interdisciplinary sites" that bring "into focus networks and relations of power, resistance, histories, and the everyday, rather than locations that are simply subjugated, perpetually ghettoized, or ungeographic."[23]

## Historical Geographies of Development

My focus on how local, Black USDA agents in the Jim Crow South negotiated the terrain of the USDA's biopolitical mandate in an attempt to support Black farmers adds a perspective to the historical geographies of contemporary development that foregrounds the significance of the plantation to that genealogy and highlights how top-down development projects are resisted and at times transformed by local actors. Most scholars interrogating the historical roots of contemporary U.S. development practices focus on large state-run projects of technoscience during the interwar and postwar periods, including the Tennessee Valley Authority's impact on African infrastructural investments, the U.S. Bureau of Reclamations dam-building projects throughout the tricontinental world, and the Rockefeller Foundation's green revolution in Mexico and later India.[24] These scientific and economic modernizations strategies that served as tools of the Cold War are certainly important sites for understanding the U.S.'s later technological aid efforts throughout the 1960s and 1970s. But as Duffield argues, these forms of development are distinct from a countermovement among the U.S. political elites, an attitude to development that was "enshrined in the 'small is beautiful' approach to local sustainability."[25] This approach, Duffield argues, forms the basis of today's liberal forms of development such as humanitarian aid and other self-help schemes.

Yet until recently, the historical geography of this countermovement has been poorly understood. Daniel Immerwahr's recent investigation of what he calls "community development" traces the "small is beautiful" approach to some key thinkers and policymakers active in the 1930s Franklin D. Roosevelt administration and documents how this communitarian impulse that provided a counter to modernization theories influenced U.S. foreign interventions, particularly in India and the Philippines.[26] His focus on policymakers at the top and on circles of communication centered on Washington, D.C., provides an important context for understanding the roots of liberal forms of development, but leaves unexamined the ways in which those forms were actually practiced in a particular place and on a particular group of racialized people, and the ways in which those people through their everyday actions enacted, translated, and transformed those policies. This book argues that those grounded practices and particulars matter. They matter for the obvious reasons; that development, however conceived, impacts peoples' lives in specific ways, and those stories matter to the affected communities and families. But they matter too in the intellectual history and geography of development. The statements of policymakers and of other influential elites regarding development work are often voiced as lofty goals with only vague outlines of how those goals are to be implemented. They rarely offer insights into how racialized and gendered norms matter in implementing those goals and how local actors like Laura Daly negotiated between those lofty goals and the realities of an oppressive and racist local state that disenfranchised and impoverished those they were meant to help. In other words, by focusing on the elite managers of development, and ignoring the racist and gendered context in which community development projects unfolded, scholars have overlooked a fundamental component of many liberal development schemes, and that is their roots in the plantation and the anti-Black racism and violence that undergirded it.

Liberal development schemes certainly differed from the large, modernization projects referenced earlier, but both schemes were tools of geoeconomics and geopolitics. As scholars from a range of disciplines have shown, the demands of capitalism to accumulate profits through control over land, resources, and people fueled both large-scale modernization projects and small-scale community development schemes.[27] Many liberal development projects, guided by the principles of self-help and community-building, were geared toward creating, maintaining, and controlling a stable, inexpensive agricultural workforce. These projects, as scholars have forcefully shown, are grounded in the logic and practices of the plantation, a system that relied on racialized, involuntary labor.[28] Laura Daly may not have been confronting the horrors of chattel slavery, but as I will make clear in the following section, the sharecropping and tenant farming system in which she lived and worked relied on coerced labor. Anti-Black racism, amplified through the Atlantic slave trade that relegated Black people to the realm of the nonhuman, enabled and legitimized this system that reaped billions of dollars in profit to white landowners and merchants.[29] And when cotton production and other forms of plantation agriculture moved outside the United States, the logic and practices of the plantation—racialized violence and coerced labor—moved with it.[30] So by centering my analysis on the practices of people like Daly and how racism operated in the Jim Crow South, instead of on white elite actors who guided community development policies, I am able to highlight the constitutive role that racism played and plays in the long historical geography of development.

Interestingly, more explicit attention to the Jim Crow South is evident in scholarship tracing the roots of development practices within the British context and its colonial heritage, although here again the significance of the plantation to this genealogy is not addressed. Scholars have documented how colonial experts in the interwar and early postwar period drew on the model of African American education in the U.S. South in order to revamp their educational strategies by focusing on providing Africans with a basic education and training in modern agricultural techniques and other practical matters.[31] The Great Depression and war years had altered imperial imaginations, networks, and policies in significant ways, shifting how colonial officers envisioned the future role of African agriculture and peoples.[32] Administrators in the Colonial Office, for example, were encouraged to base policies on newly discovered scientific knowledge of colonial agriculture and ecology, thus impacting the development agenda overseas and scientific practices at home.[33] In Kenya, for example, that new scientific knowledge combined with the disruptions of World War II led to a greater emphasis on community-building and self-help as tools for economic and social improvement.[34] In general, as Joseph Hodge has argued, recognition of potential economic and social crises in Africa caused by an over-reliance on export-production in agriculture caused many in the Colonial Office to rethink their policies, particularly those aimed at rural education.[35] As scholars have shown, the type of education offered at places such as Tuskegee—a curriculum focused on agriculture and industry—was seen as an appropriate model of rural education.[36] Recently, scholars have begun to recognize that rural improvement projects in colonial Africa were not the result solely of Colonial Office mandates, but instead progressed through negotiations with African leaders who oftentimes had their own visions of improvement.[37] This situation is analogous to what was happening at the USDA's African American agricultural extension service in the 1920s and 1930s, where Thomas Campbell—the director of that service—and agents like Daly, were also negotiating between mandates from above and their own goals of racial uplift.[38] In examining in detail how the tensions between sometimes conflicting mandates were worked through and at times resisted in the practices of the Black USDA extension service, and in centering the constitutive role that racism played in rural development schemes in the U.S. South, this book widens and complicates the comparison between British colonial practices in Africa and U.S. improvement projects in the South.

My focus on those negotiations is not intended to imply that they occurred on a negotiating table with each side equally represented, like our commonplace understanding of that term would have it. Drawing on the work of scholars of intersectionality, I know that as a Black woman living in Alabama in the first half of the twentieth century, Daly experienced the "interlocking violence of racism, patriarchy, heteronormativity, and capitalism" that characterized the Jim Crow South.[39] Racial and sexual oppression determined most of her life's choices, including where and how she could live and work and what people she identified as family and community. However, to acknowledge this is not to say that her life and work were completely defined by what Katherine McKittrick calls plantation geographies, that is, the sociospatial structures that "normalized black dispossession, white supremacy, and other colonial-racial geographies."[40] As McKittrick and others in the field of Black geographies have made clear, to assume that Daly's life and work were contained by these oppressions is to cause another act of injustice; that is, it would deny agency and therefore humanity to Daly, reenacting racial logics and in McKittrick's word, overtaxing the "suffering black body."[41] Therefore throughout this book I have done my best to understand Daly and her fellow Black USDA agents as occupying complex and at times contradictory subject positions: as USDA agents they were granted state power to intervene in the lives of others; as Black people living in the Jim Crow South, they were the objects of those interventions. Nonetheless, the importance of those plantation geographies in shaping the life and work of Daly and her fellow agents cannot be overstated, and so in the next section I outline the context in which USDA African American agents attempted to improve and uplift poor, Black farmers.

## The USDA in the Jim Crow South

Laura Daly's home demonstration work was funded through the USDA's cooperative extension program, a program whose overall aim was to modernize U.S. agriculture through mechanization and the introduction and adoption of "scientific" forms of farming. Since the late nineteenth century, the U.S. government sought mechanisms to promote modernized farming and other practical skills through partnerships with what ultimately came to be called land-grant universities—so-called because these institutions were granted federal lands that they could use to raise funds.[42] Originally one institution was chosen as the land-grant per state, but in the South this meant that only white people had access to these federally supported programs. In 1890, institutions like Tuskegee that had been founded to provide higher education for African Americans were granted land-grant status and received some federal dollars, in effect creating a second tier of land-grant colleges throughout the South.[43] The passage of the Smith-Lever Act in 1914 formalized the relationship between the USDA and land-grant universities to conduct outreach activities in order to modernize farming and farm life throughout the United States through the USDA's extension service.[44] The USDA's agricultural extension service was comprised of three divisions with distinct goals: Farm Demonstration Work was meant to help men modernize their farming techniques; Home Demonstration Work (HDW) was meant to improve homemaking skills for women; and 4-H was designed to develop children into modern future farmers and farmwives. As scholars have shown, the exact nature of the type of work USDA agents actually conducted varied according to region and timeframe, and as county, state, regional, and national directors shifted their priorities.[45] And as I've noted earlier, it also varied according to racial categories. The USDA's extension service, like all agencies of the federal government, was racially segregated. In the U.S. South, this meant that there were in effect not three divisions (farm, home, 4-H) but six.

Southern farming was singled out by the USDA as particularly backward and in need of modernization given its reliance on human instead of technological labor.[46] Both the myth and the reality of the devastation that was being caused by the boll weevil, a small beetle that feeds on cotton buds and flowers and that had spread from Mexico into Texas and then east in the early years of the twentieth century, provided USDA agents with a problem that was in need of governmental interventions.[47] Diversification of farming was seen as key to battling the boll weevil, as was teaching better plowing and harvesting techniques, and the USDA through its state and local agents developed an infrastructure for spreading this message to southern farmers.

The USDA was particularly interested in places like Montgomery and Macon counties, Alabama, counties that constituted the heart of the Cotton Belt. Originally the land of the Muscogee Creek people before they were forcibly moved to Oklahoma by the federal government in the 1830s, the area was taken by white farmers in the early nineteenth century and divided into large cotton plantations.[48] Emancipation may have ended slavery, but it did little to change the conditions under which most African Americans lived. Clyde Woods reminds us that in the post-Reconstruction period, "the remnants of autonomy [of African-Americans] were destroyed as planters tried to extract more labor for less and less compensation."[49] As economists and historians have shown, sharecropping and tenant farming relied on the labor-repressive system of the plantation, one that tied laborers to the land through a set of legal, economic, and social mechanisms of control that Bobby Wilson has referred to as the "peculiar institution of southern tenancy."[50] The most important of those mechanisms was debt peonage, a system whereby tenant farmers and sharecroppers were never able to repay the debts that they had incurred through the planting and harvesting season. Bound through contracts that required tenants and sharecroppers to make overdue payments only by staying on the land and farming another year or be sentenced to labor gangs, this mechanism legally tied farm workers to the land that they worked.[51] Described as a "characteristic feature of cotton agriculture in the postwar South," some studies estimate that 80 percent of sharecroppers in Alabama were held under such conditions.

Additionally, most states in the South passed a series of laws that limited the mobility of its workforce. Enticement statutes made it a criminal offense for one landlord to entice workers away from another, while emigrant agent laws provided severe restrictions on out-of-state agents' abilities to recruit labor. Laws were also enacted that made it a crime for workers to break their contracts, and according to the criminal justice system, if convicted of breaking their contracts they would be sentenced to work, often back on the plantation. And a series of variously construed vagrancy laws basically ceded to the criminal justice system the right to arrest people wherever and whenever they were not working.[52] These laws and practices that tied African Americans to agricultural land and labor were underwritten by Jim Crow laws that provided legal sanction to the racial segregation of public spaces.[53] And of course all of these mechanisms that were meant to keep Black people in place—that is, working on plantations—were reinforced by the constant fear of violence from the Ku Klux Klan and others. In essence, the postbellum South's agricultural system relied on involuntary servitude in order to maintain its profitability; and at the heart of that servitude were spatial constraints on the mobility of agricultural laborers.

Let me illustrate by relating two interesting stories that appeared side-by-side in the 1919 edition of the *Negro Year Book*, an encyclopedic publication edited by Monroe Work and published by Tuskegee Institute that was comprised of news features, short essays, and statistical summaries that were meant to encapsulate the state of African Americans during the preceding year. In this case, that year (1917–1918) was noteworthy, covering the United States' participation in World War I and the related migration of Black labor North. The first story summarizes a movement initiated at Tuskegee and later endorsed by the USDA to enlist Black farmers in the South to work six days a week instead of five so as to provide more food and materials for the war effort. Called the Saturday Service League, it discouraged men from taking Saturdays off by appealing to their patriotism and duty. As Dr. Robert M. Moton, president of Tuskegee, wrote in his plea: "Would you let a single American die from hunger when it was within your power to share a crust with him? Yet every time you waste food, every time you neglect your garden and crop you are snatching bread out of the mouth of the American Soldier."[54] The subsequent story discussed the governments' "work or fight" law (a rule initiated by the War Department in 1918 that threatened unemployed men with immediate draft into the military) that was being used to force African Americans into what Work called a "condition of virtual peonage" since "the War Department's ruling applied only to men subject to the draft, whereas, the locally enacted laws were in their enforcement made to apply to persons of all ages, and in most cases to women."[55] Work's sense of injustice is apparent in the detailed example he provides: "A colored woman was arrested for not working. She told the court at her trial that she was married, that her husband earned enough to enable her to stay at home and take care of the home and her children and these duties kept her too busy to do any other work. Despite this statement, she was fined $25.75 and told by the court that she 'would either work in service or on the public works' as being married did not exempt her from the provisions of the law.'"[56] As the first article suggests, the need for agricultural labor was so strong, and the sight of idle African Americans so threatening, that some African Americans felt compelled to work even on Saturdays, while the second piece demonstrates that those needs and threats trumped even gendered norms.

The late nineteenth and early twentieth centuries witnessed Progressive-era reforms to the social fabric of cities in the North, suffrage movements for women, recognition of the rights of industrial workers to unionize and strike, and the mechanization of many forms of agriculture, particularly in the grain-producing regions of the North and West.[57] But the agricultural system of the Mississippi Delta and the Black Belt of Alabama, a system that was made possible and profitable through debt peonage, spatial controls over labor, and constant surveillance, remained stubbornly intact.[58] Yet in the late 1910s and early 1920s a set of crises were perceived to be threatening this system, crises that were precipitated by the Great Migration,[59] and that centered on the bodies and well-being of Black agricultural laborers. The legal, social, and spatial restraints that had kept people in place were proving inadequate in the face of what was perceived to be an acute labor shortage. At stake was the production and sale of the United States' largest agricultural export—cotton—worth, according to the USDA, $1,136,468,916 in 1920.[60] It was within this context that the USDA, through its partners at Tuskegee Institute and Alabama Polytechnic Institute, attempted to intervene in order to modernize southern farming. How, then, did African American agents like Laura Daly proceed?

**Structure of the Book**

As a USDA home demonstration agent, Daly sent her annual reports to the head of the State of Alabama's Cooperative Extension Service based at Auburn Polytechnic Institute, at first John F. Duggar and later Luther Duncan when he was appointed head in 1920. But her daily life and work unfolded at Tuskegee, and her de facto supervisor was Thomas M. Campbell. Campbell, who had graduated from Tuskegee, was appointed as the first Black agricultural agent in 1906 and moved up the ranks to become the state agent and eventually the agent of the USDA in charge of African American extension for the district that included the Black Belt of Georgia and Alabama and the Mississippi Delta.[61] This book documents and analyzes three strategies developed by Campbell and his fellow USDA agents as they attempted to fit the USDA's mandate of modernizing agriculture into the contours of the Jim Crow South, while staying true to their belief in racial uplift.

No doubt greatly influenced by his education at Tuskegee and well aware of the impoverished status of Black farmers, Campbell and other USDA officials began to gradually shape the USDA's mandate—to modernize agriculture—into practices that could provide assistance to Black farmers in the form of health, sanitation, home improvement, and home and land ownership. Chapter 2 examines the ways in which home demonstration agents like Laura Daly negotiated between federal-level mandates that were meant to shape women into "proper" housewives, and a system that required those women to act as men; that is, as farm laborers. This almost impossible subject position—what Sarah Haley refers to as the "unbearable flexibility of nonbeing"—meant that Black home demonstration workers were faced daily with mandates that simply could not be fulfilled.[62] As a result, Daly and others shifted their priorities. In other words, this chapter documents how—particularly in the 1920s— Black home demonstration agents began to practice their work differently from white agents. Based primarily on analyses of USDA's county and state agents' reports in the 1910s and 1920s in Alabama and Mississippi, I show how home improvements directed at white women shifted their emphasis from home production—particularly food and clothing—to home consumption. In other words, and following the trend of the emerging field of home economics, home demonstration work directed at white women focused on teaching them how to become more knowledgeable consumers of domestic products. In contrast, Black home demonstration agents deepened their focus on home production particularly regarding food, with an increased emphasis on teaching farm women to become better food and health providers for their families. In this way the agents provided basic support for Black farm women and their families—what Beverly Mullings has called "life-work"—while either ignoring or translating the new consumerist mandates to align with the constraints/contradictions of Black consumer culture in the Jim Crow South.[63] These interventions, I argue, were tolerated (and sometimes encouraged) by federal-level USDA bureaucrats given the anxieties of plantation owners and other white elites in the Cotton Belt and elsewhere over the declining numbers and health of their Black agricultural labor force. At the same time, these practices attended to the anxieties of many Black leaders and employees at the USDA who saw daily the costs of poverty to the health and well-being of their community.

Home demonstration work, however, was only one small piece of the USDA's extension service's operations and was limited in terms of its impact for a variety of reasons. As I discussed earlier, most Black farmers lived under conditions of debt peonage, tied through legal and other means to the plantations where they worked.[64] Without legal access to land and with few other resources, sharecroppers and tenant farm families were in no position to modernize their farming technologies or homemaking skills. Chapter 3 traces how local officials at Tuskegee responded to this situation by developing a new technique for educating farm families—what was called the movable school—a mobile form of intervention that brought improvements literally to the farmers with immediate effects. At first a wagon and later a truck, the movable school scheduled demonstrations at farms throughout the areas surrounding Tuskegee, thus eliminating the need for farmers to travel to Tuskegee and delivering education without the cumbersome apparatus of club meetings. Although originally staffed by two local USDA agents, a nurse was added in 1923 to both dispense medical help and to conduct lessons on home sanitation, health, and disease. In effect this amounted to what we today would call a traveling nurse program, providing for most Black farmers their only access to medical care. The movable school, in other words, was a delivery system for providing basic assistance to farm families.

What I show in chapter 3 are the ways in which the movable school became the symbol for and enactment of successful uplift and development. Local USDA agents based at Tuskegee considered the movable school a showpiece for all of their extension work and used it to garner positive publicity and funding. Visitors to Tuskegee—northern philanthropists, missionaries, social scientists—were often taken out to rural areas to see for themselves the work of the movable school. Drawing on Field's notion of the aesthetics of uplift,[65] I analyze the various representations of the movable school—a 1921 USDA film, first-person accounts, official reports, photographs, and a book written by Campbell—and outline the ways in which they adopted a rhetorical structure of before-and-after sequencing that reinforced the legitimacy of the discourse of uplift, and therefore the legitimacy of Tuskegee and the USDA's African American extension service. With the threat of the "before" image haunting these representations, the act of uplift was presented as ongoing into the future, always in process without end. In this way, these enactments of racial uplift did not present a direct threat to the status quo of white supremacy.

Both African American home demonstration work and the movable school emphasized the survival of Black agricultural life through attention to food production, health, and living conditions, strategies through which USDA extension service local officials could funnel federal dollars and potentially help farmers. But the structural constraints of tenant farming and sharecropping meant that little could be done to improve their economic standing. For that, Black farmers would need to own their own land. In chapter 4, I document various schemes developed by Tuskegee and local USDA officials to make it possible for African American farmers to own homes and land, schemes that culminated in the 1936 Prairie Farms Resettlement community. With the long reach of the federal government administered through Tugwell's Resettlement Administration (RA), Tuskegee officials proposed the buyout of a tract of land owned by absentee landlords that was labeled "submarginal"; the tenants working the land would be resettled elsewhere, with those deemed "worthy" given the option of buying their own land through mortgages made available from the government. Between 1935 and 1938, these two interrelated schemes—the Tuskegee Land Utilization Project, and Prairie Farms Resettlement Project—uprooted and relocated more than six hundred people living near Tuskegee in Macon County with the goal of improving their lives through creating self-sustaining farms, homes, and communities.[66]

Yet as I highlight in chapter 4, the idea of moving tenant farmers to better land and encouraging land ownership was not new to Macon County or Tuskegee Institute. Prairie Farms was simply one of a series of many experiments in resettling Black farmers. From the early 1900s onward, Tuskegee officials and Black USDA agents, with the help of northern philanthropists, had created a succession of model African American farming communities. All of these communities included the construction of homes and schools and provided funding for eventual home and land ownership.[67] The Resettlement Administration's emphasis on countering land degradation simply added an additional metric—soil erosion—to the calculus of where Black farmers could live. Chapter 4 analyzes the ways in which Tuskegee officials attempted to meld their ideal of racial uplift to the RA's and later Farm Security Administration's mandates of creating better farmland and farm communities, all the while being aware of the limitations to that improvement within the structure of white supremacy. It documents how local and regional white officials found the farmers at Prairie Farms not adhering to their correct roles as patriarchal, heteronormative farm families, while the community was deemed unworthy of future investment.

Chapter 5 investigates how many of the strategies devised by Laura Daly and other employees of the USDA's African American extension service were folded into plans for postwar reconstruction overseas. I do so by analyzing two events that occurred in 1944. The first was a conference sponsored by the USDA's extension service whose goal was to begin planning for overseas extension work in the countries that had suffered war-related destruction in rural areas. I show how the conference and its successor (in 1949) focused rural reconstruction efforts on home and community development rather than technological aid, while emphasizing the significance of a healthy population to the stability of the new postwar consensus. The second event I analyze is a survey that Thomas Campbell (along with two others) conducted in West Africa from late 1944 through early 1945, querying why he was chosen to participate. I trace his literal route from Tuskegee to West Africa, his visits to various educational and missionary facilities accompanied by Jackson Davis and Margaret Wrong, and his return home via England, Scotland, and Washington, D.C. in order to discuss with British colonial administrators and USDA officials the results of the survey. Through archival documentation of the trip and an interrogation of the book *Africa Advancing* that was written after, I show that it was Campbell's experience with and expertise in the USDA's African American extension service—his experience directing biopolitical interventions within the racist Jim Crow South—that positioned him as a potential colonial and development advisor. A letter written from the head of one of the missionary stations the group visited indicates the nature of Campbell's contributions to the survey: "The people who met you were happy for the privilege and you possibly did more good than you know. If our people here will be able to grasp the idea that they can do a lot for themselves if they put themselves to it, it will be a new day.... The things that were said at Battenburg Hall by Mr. Campbell sank rather deep. Coming from a man who is doing just that sort of thing, it was an eye opener to some of the people. I only wish you could have gone to a great many stations up country and talked to the people there."[68] In other words, I show that what marked Campbell as *the* person to co-direct the survey was his more than thirty years of experience overseeing the USDA's Black agricultural extension service, getting people to "grasp the idea that they can do a lot for themselves if they put themselves to it." Documentation of both 1944 events reveals how some of the practices devised by Daly and Campbell were carried forward into overseas reconstruction efforts, while others—particularly those that would threaten land tenure arrangements—were not.

I conclude by returning to Tuskegee and the lives of Laura Daly and Thomas Campbell. In 1944, Daly was appointed a representative of the Consumer Division of the United States' Office of Price Administration for a brief time, before returning to the USDA's extension service. Campbell too, returned to Tuskegee after his African trip, continuing to direct the USDA's African American extension service until retirement. As some of the practices that they and their fellow agents had created were being used as models for development efforts in India and parts of Africa, their roots in the U.S. South and among Black farmers were forgotten and ignored as they were disembedded from the politics of racial uplift. Community development and rural improvement became projects directed by white experts and undertaken by white men and women who practiced village-level interventions on racialized peoples, continuing the long history of plantation geographies.

## CHAPTER 2

# Home Demonstration Work and the Sustaining of Black Life

In her 1929 annual report summarizing the work completed by the fifteen Black home demonstrators in Alabama, Luella Hanna highlighted the importance of home improvement for what she calls the "advancements of all people." "A good, clean comfortable and convenient home with tasty furnishings is one of the fundamental necessities in the cultural, social and economic advancements of all people," she writes, adding that "this has been sadly neglected as far as the rural Negro is concerned." Her explanation of that neglect is telling: "Economic pressure has caused him to convert his would be 'housekeepers' or 'home makers' into producers of corn and cotton—mostly cotton. It has been the home demonstration agent's task to instill in the hearts and minds of every club woman and girl (and at the same time convert the men) that they are the present and future 'home makers and help mates' for present and future homes and husbands."[1] In this quote, Hanna puts her finger directly on the quagmire faced by Black home demonstration agents working in the Cotton Belt of the Jim Crow South: how to align the mandate of the USDA's extension service with the realities—or as she says, the "necessities"—of a system that required women to work as farm laborers. In this way she is giving voice to an issue that has haunted the subject position of Black women from the time of enslavement onward, what Sarah Haley refers to as the "unbearable flexibility of nonbeing."[2] In other words, agents like Hanna had to negotiate between mandates meant to help shape women into "proper" housewives, within a system that required those women to act as men; that is, as farm laborers. For Haley, this impossible flexibility of subject positions constituted and reinforced Black women as nonhuman.

And yet, as scholars have argued, the value accrued by Black women's labor in the realm of social reproduction—that is, their work to sustain family and community, what Beverly Mullings has called "life-work"—is critically important as it was the only form of value that could not be appropriated by plantation owners.[3] Enslaved people in the Caribbean, for example, often had access to provision grounds where they could grow their own food and at times sell it at markets, thus allowing for the endurance of networks of knowledge and practice that allowed them to "survive the brutality of the system."[4] These spaces that were both "within the order dictated by the plantation and yet detached from it" were critical to creating and maintaining practices of living as free people, ultimately allowing for the formation of social and political solidarities that shaped resistance movements throughout the enslaved world.[5] Given the unfree labor system that characterized the Cotton Belt of the Jim Crow South—what Blackmon has called "slavery by another name"—I argue in this chapter that the job of home demonstration agents like Hanna and Laura Daly was its own form of life-work, providing Black tenant and sharecropping families with value in the form of structures of knowledges and practices in regard to food, clothing, and health care that could not be appropriated by their landlords.[6] As Black women themselves working on a daily basis with other Black women, Hanna and Laura Daly understood the almost impossible realities women faced, laboring at home and in the fields, and the importance of this additional labor to the survival of Black life and community. This chapter documents how they helped women accomplish this work. Building on scholarship that has documented the long history of Black women's tireless contributions to sustaining Black life, this chapter examines how Hanna and Daly quietly ignored the USDA's Home Demonstration Unit as its goals shifted toward the realm of home economics and so-called rational consumption, instead doubling-down on their efforts to maintain practices of life-work that challenged the plantation order.[7] By so doing, they engaged in their own form of resistance.

### Home Demonstration Work

What was called the Home Demonstration Unit of the USDA's agricultural extension service was one of several such Progressive-era movements to reform and modernize people through interventions that focused on home and home practices. The program drew on but differed from two other efforts in the United States that targeted the home and domesticity as sites of sociospatial interventions. The first program—the Bureau of Indian Affairs' "field matrons"—was similar in its commitment to the home and the domestic sphere as sites of intervention, but it relied primarily on Victorian notions of proper femininity not Progressive-era reform politics. From 1890 to 1938, white, middle-class field matrons were sent to live on reservations primarily in the Great Plains in order to "civilize" Native Americans through introducing Anglo American norms of femininity.[8] Native women were meant to forego their former lives as economic participants in their communities in order to become Victorian housewives.[9] Coincident with these interventions in the American West were those sponsored principally by private organizations in the East and Midwest aimed at "assimilating" immigrants into American middle-class, white society through teaching women how to become "modern" housewives. The settlement house movement that had begun in mid-nineteenth century London with efforts to overcome socioeconomic class divides through providing education at neighborhood-based centers or "houses" was transformed most famously by Jane Addams at Hull House in Chicago to address what the U.S. elites assumed to be the problem of fitting immigrants into normalized modes of American life. Addams and other reformers in early twentieth century America focused on immigrant women and children, providing classes on such skills as "proper" cooking, cleaning, and clothing for women, and providing recreational and sport activities for children with the assumption that that these skills would help transform foreigners into white, middle-class Americans.[10]

The home demonstration work (HDW) of the USDA shared the primary assumption of these two programs: that a key to transforming groups of people thought not to be part of the white, U.S., middle-class was modernizing and making more scientific the domestic and all that went with it: food preparation, sanitation and health, textile and clothing production, and home management and maintenance. Like the settlement house movement, it brought together Progressive-era reformist impulses with the emerging field of home economics, and drew on and contributed to the emergence of the suffrage movement.[11] But because home demonstration work was part of a national-scale agricultural extension program, and in 1923 was institutionally recognized with the formation of the Bureau of Home Economics, a division of the USDA, the impact of this program was national in scope.[12] Originating in the southern states, women were first employed on an ad hoc basis by local and state-run agricultural extension offices to oversee girls' canning clubs, community organizations meant to teach young women the latest scientific methods of canning food.[13] The 1914 Smith-Lever Act provided federal appropriations for women trained in home economics to work alongside the county agents, funding that was augmented by a combination of support from state land-grant universities, and local businesses and organizations. By 1933, the USDA estimated that more than a million farm women were active members of groups organized by home demonstration agents.[14]

Whereas the goals of the farm demonstration program focused on improving and making more productive farm outputs through adopting scientifically proven methods of cultivation and using modern technology, the explicit and implicit goals of the Home Demonstration Unit were far more complex. The discipline of home economics that informed home demonstration work began in the late nineteenth century as a movement to bring scientific rationality to home management, aligning with agricultural reform movements that focused on modernizing farm management. Yet as Carolyn Goldstein has shown, in the interwar period, home economics and domestic rural intervention programs like HDW began to coalesce around the notion of creating the rational consumer: "In contrast to 19th century domestic scientists who emphasized efficient production within the home, the first generation of home economists shaped their movement to address the growing importance of consumption for the nation's homemakers at the turn of the century. Home economics found support for this social and cultural agenda from Progressive educational leaders and reformers looking to modernize agriculture and all aspects of rural life."[15] Goldstein detects the shift in home economics from an emphasis on home production to home consumption through an analysis of the discipline's proponents who worked in government agencies such as the Bureau of Home Economics and those who worked in business, advising corporations in the new field of consumer behavior.

The USDA's Home Demonstration Unit was certainly informed by this transformation. As the senior home economist for the extension service wrote in her 1933 summary of home demonstration work, "To meet these needs ways must be found to do the tasks of the home with a minimum of labor and time and to devise sources of income that will enable the home maker to purchase those things that will make for efficiency, comfort, and attractiveness."[16] Yet for women who conducted HDW, working literally on the ground in rural, often poor areas of the country, attention to the immediate needs of providing food and adequate housing often outweighed training in so-called rational consumption.[17] And this was particularly true for Black home demonstrators who were often working with sharecropping or tenant farm families in the South; women working with women who had neither the time nor resources to devote to consumption and whose status as "nonbeings" was produced through what was considered their ever-flexible identities (manual laborers, proper housewives, heteronormative women).

In addition, Black women's involvement in consumption was curtailed not only by their limited resources but also by the white elite who perceived Black access to commodities as threatening to the racial order.[18] As Bobby Wilson has outlined, the system of commodity exchange in the postbellum South was fraught with contradictions. No longer legally bound as commodities themselves, postbellum Black farmers and laborers were free to purchase their own commodities, and as capitalists, southern entrepreneurs and merchants were always looking to expand their markets. Yet this freedom upset the racial hierarchy. As Wilson argues, "free to engage in the circuit of commodity exchange and consumption, former slaves did not abide by the old standard of passive behavior. They created new social geographies by moving and crossing the rigid boundary drawn by slavery."[19] These new behaviors and geographies threatened the rigid order of white supremacy, as did the potential equality offered through the availability of similar products to whites and Blacks, purchased in the same spaces of consumption, such as department stores. Wilson argues that a spatial-racial fix solved this potential contradiction in commodity capitalism—segregation: "segregation provided capital access to the black market without violating the racial order, making white supremacy compatible with the interest of businesses."[20] So even if African American farmwomen had extra money to spend, their participation in the consumer economy was limited by the segregated access to transportation and shopping spaces and the norms of acceptable Black behavior and appearance. Home demonstrators like Luella Hanna and Laura Daly, therefore, were confronting an array of obstacles to the promotion of rational consumption. Black tenant farmers relied on their landlord's supply store or commissary to purchase their goods, and those goods were almost always overpriced and of low quality, while Black farm owners had limited, segregated, and degraded access to supplies in town.[21] What I explore in this chapter is how home demonstrators like Luella Hanna and Laura Daly, facing the mandates for consumer education from above and the needs for direct assistance in the provisioning of food and health care from below, began to forge their own path that resonated with the needs of the women and families they worked with.[22]

## White Home Demonstration Work

Like all other parts of the extension service operating in southern states, home demonstration work was segregated: each state employed white women as county home demonstration agents to attend to the needs of white farm women, and Black women to serve as demonstration agents for Black farm women.[23] And even though the USDA's mandate for what was to be accomplished in both white and Black home demonstration work was identical, the actual practices of each began to differ throughout the 1920s. The practices of white home demonstration workers accorded with Goldstein's analysis; that is, their work began to shift from an emphasis on creating better home producers to molding more informed home consumers, while the work of Black home demonstration agents maintained its emphasis on home production, particularly food, while augmenting it with attention to health care.

As noted previously, in its early years before federal funding was allocated, HDW consisted primarily of volunteer interventions by prominent women community leaders who often formed clubs to share their knowledge of new food preservation technologies, particularly the canning of fruits and vegetables from their gardens (fig. 2.1). With more mandated federal funding after the passage of the Smith-Lever Act, the work expanded into other forms of homemaking. For example, the 1915 annual report for HDW in the State of Alabama made repeated reference to demonstrations of correct canning techniques for either fruits or vegetables and the best ways to construct and use what was called a fireless cooker.[24] Fireless cookers were similar to what we today would call a slow cooker; a pot of food was heated by a stove or fire and then placed in some sort of metal pot that was covered tightly and surrounded with insulating materials such as sawdust or soapstone and allowed to simmer for long periods of time. This was considered a far more economical, time saving (one could do other activities while cooking) potentially safer (given that many rural women did not have access to stoves) way to cook. Some limited attention was given to health-related issues such as fly traps and house screens. A survey of annual reports on home demonstration work reveals similar activities, primarily focused on home production.[25]

As the organization became more robust through the next decade or so, this initial focus on canning and cooking was augmented with attention to other forms of food production and health. Mary Feminear, the state agent for Alabama, divided the work done for the year 1919 into two categories: agriculture and home economics. For the former category she writes, "In the work in Agriculture in the past year stress was placed upon gardening, poultry raising, and home orchards." She categorized the work of home economics as consisting of five main areas: study of foods and cookery, food preparation, health, clothing, and home improvement and beautification. Her description of what was involved in health activities was the longest, and she lists the "health problems" that were "studied and discussed": home sanitation, extermination of pests, water supply, sanitary toilets, communicable diseases, typhoid and malaria, and milk and its relationship to disease.[26]

**FIGURE 2.1.** Women and girls of the Mabelvale Home Demonstration Club posed around their home canned goods, Pulaski County, Arkansas, 1912. University of Arkansas Agricultural Extension Service Records, Mabelvale Home Demonstration Club Records, box 5, Special Collections, University of Arkansas Libraries, Fayetteville.

Yet alongside these concerns was an increasing attention to consumption. By the late teens and early 1920s, pamphlets were produced by home demonstration agents offering advice about how best to launder clothes, to cook and clean proficiently (often through using new technologies), and to buy and arrange furniture, carpets, and drapes.[27] And the annual reports sent to Washington D.C. began to include lengthy discussions of home and community beautification projects, landscape gardening, and interior design. By 1930, Anne E. Jordan, a home demonstration specialist in Mississippi reported on the results of her living-room campaign: "The aim of this campaign is to help club members and other women to have an attractive and comfortable room for the family to enjoy every day and for guests. The cold dark parlor, wide drafty hall, cluttered bedroom, or little used dining room may become a 'livable living room' with little expense and few changes."[28] So the duties of white home demonstration agents included teaching farm women how to become modern citizen-consumers in addition to training them in the basic skills of home production of food and clothing. For many of them, their duties also included supervising their African American peers. In her 1921 report, Alabama home demonstration agent Mary Killebrew wrote that "it is also my duty to supervise the Negro Demonstration Work."[29] Summarizing thirty years of home demonstration work in Mississippi, May Cresswell (1944) explains: "Part of the duty of white home demonstration agents is the supervision and direction of work among negro families by negro home demonstration agents. White leaders stand ready to give encouragement and support to the negro home demonstration agents in their efforts to lead negro families toward a better, more healthful, more wholesome way of life."[30]

Yet as I will explain in the next sections, throughout the 1920s as white home demonstration work became increasingly geared toward training farm women to become modern consumers, Black home demonstration work, under the "guidance" first of white demonstration agents and later supervised from Tuskegee, began to crystallize around interventions aimed at improving food production and bodily health. In other words, although the mandates from the federal office were identical, the practices of white home demonstration work and Black home demonstration work diverged. Those differences emerged in the late 1910s and 1920s, as white home demonstration work switched its focus to creating better citizen-consumers, while Black home demonstration work continued its strong emphasis on helping women to fulfill their families' basic needs, those of social reproduction: food production and preservation, health, childcare, and home sanitation.

## Black Home Demonstration Work

In her 1919 annual report, N. Juanita Coleman, the African American home demonstration agent for Macon County, replies to the question "What is the most effective work done?" with: "The making and using of the fireless cookers. During the planting and gathering of the farm crops, the majority of my club members assist their husbands with this work during this season. The food is hurriedly or in most cases poorly prepared. Through the aid of the fireless cooker the housewife has been able to work right along, going home with the family, instead of the fry dinner she has given a real wholesome meal. In some cases the cooker is carried to the field, dinner is served at work under the trees."[31] Coleman and other Black home demonstration agents turned to technologies like the fireless cooker because it allowed women to work in the fields and at the same time prepare meals. In this way, it satisfied both the gendered ideals of womanhood as set forth in the separate spheres ideology that dominated the late nineteenth and early twentieth centuries, and also the needs of the white landowners. In her description of how demonstrations in regard to the fireless cooker were particularly appropriate during the early summer months, a local agent aptly and succinctly touted its benefits "since the wives and daughters are field hands as well as housekeepers."[32] And, as my analyses of Black home demonstration reports throughout the 1920s shows, this was indeed its focus: helping Black women and girls become better housekeepers measured in terms of meeting the immediate needs of their family, while always mindful that these same women were also conducting farm labor.

In her 1920 report of her work that she had completed as the agent in charge of home demonstrations with the movable school (for more about the movable school see chapter 3), Coleman wrote that her job varied by season, and included instruction on gardening, food preparation and preservation including the use of the fireless cooker, and home nursing.[33] The one constant was attention to sanitation, health, and children. "Throughout the year," Coleman writes, home demonstration work stressed "sanitation, conservation of energy, food and time, and the care of children."[34] That attention to health and sanitation continued throughout the decade. Summarizing her work as the state agent for Black women in Alabama, Luella Hanna wrote in 1928 that "Health and sanitation in the home of our rural people has been and is now quite a problem for the home demonstration agents. This is especially true in the homes of tenant farmers, and on the farms where women and children (those who are large enough) are counted as year-round farm hands."[35]

Black home demonstration agents were constantly in situations that required them to adapt the USDA's extension service mandates—training women to become better housewives—to the realities of a situation in which most women were farm laborers barely able to meet the demands of their white landlords let alone fulfill the duties of the new consumer-citizen set out by dominant norms of early twentieth-century womanhood. And even if they did have time and resources to conduct consumer activities, they were confronted with the realities of segregation and the restrictions on Black social behavior and appearance. The above quote also suggests that the situation of Black rural children was similar to women; their roles as farm laborers conflicted with the norms of Progressive-era middle-class life that situated them as subjects for education, not manual labor.[36] The few extension service agents who worked with Black children noted the difficulties of trying to fulfill USDA mandates. The author of a 1920 report on the state of boys' clubs puts his finger directly on the problem: "Through observation I find that there are two problems that predominate in retarding the progress of club work among the Negro boys, 1) In most cases boys who are secured to do club work are the sons of tenant farmers, whose own time as well as that of the boy, in most cases, is

FIGURE 2.2. Laura R. Daly demonstrating canning techniques to a group of women. Original caption: "Can all you can—the motto of the Club Members of Montgomery County." L. C. Hanna, "Annual Report for Negro Women, State of Alabama, Year Ending Dec. 31, 1928." ACES Collection, box 356. Courtesy of Auburn University Libraries Special Collections and Archives.

mortgaged to the land-lord. Most of these boys make an excellent beginning, but as soon as the main crop begins to need work, all of the boy's time is taken to assist in [the work], 2) the other problem referred to above is that of the parents taking the products of the boy's project."[37] Children, in other words, were often unable to be "proper" boys and girls. They were little different from their parents, "mortgaged to the land-lord" as laborers, with the fruits of their labor required to support their families.

Confronted with the seemingly impossible task of teaching Black rural women and children how to become better housewives and proper boys and girls, agents like Laura Daly, then, took the USDA's mandates and funds and used them to offer practical assistance to rural families. A set of photographs that accompanied the 1928 annual report for African American women for the State of Alabama provide striking visual evidence of those practices.[38] Although it was not unusual for one or two snapshots to accompany these reports, this set of photographs are clearly not casual shots and their composition and resolution suggest they were of professional quality.[39] The photographs provide visual evidence of the practices that Black home demonstration agents had devised in order to provide useful assistance to rural farm women, practices that focused on food production, health and childcare, and home improvements. In figure 2.2, an agent is shown demonstrating canning techniques to women seated at a table outside a home, with the caption identifying the women as club members of Montgomery County. A demonstration of childcare is depicted in figure 2.3, with presumably a male doctor using a scale placed on top of a sewing cabinet and plant stand to track infant weight, a statistic considered vital to infant health, or, as the original caption says, "better babies." Several images feature home improvements, such as figure 2.4, and the before and after photos of the Jarrett family home (figures 2.5 and 2.6). Here the camera captures home improvements that turn a seemingly slovenly (clapboards are peeling off the house; the outside bench is broken; materials are scattered on the ground) and unhealthy (no screens or glass on the windows; the front door is missing) farmhouse into a tidy, well-built, and healthy house. As it turns out, and as is evident from the note at the end of the caption ("note the old house in rear") the before and after labels are misleading since the photos were taken on the same day and depict two different houses, one being completed just behind the other (for more about the use of before and after images as part of the aesthetics of uplift, see chapter 3). Notice that in the photograph of the new house the men are posed actively working on repairs, while the women chat on a porch with children looking on, properly seated on a bench instead of the broken stairs in the before image. In other words, the ideals of Progressive-era family roles have been established, in accord with the ideology of uplift. Laura Daly figures prominently in two of the photographs.[40] In figure 2.2 she is the demonstrator whose back is turned toward the camera, and, similarly, in figure 2.7 she faces away from the camera and is seated on a porch surrounded by a well-dressed family, presumably discussing possible home improvements. The focus of the photos, therefore, is clearly on the work being conducted, not on the agents or even the subjects themselves.

Importantly, the work being conducted as portrayed in these photographs deviated from the USDA's federal mandates for home extension work. For example, the before and after photos portray the work of men, while the "better babies" features a nurse and a male physician; HDW was meant to focus on women not men, and by 1928, white home demonstrators had shifted their work away from health care. Nor do any of the images depict lessons that were being offered by white agents regarding how best to make rational consumer

**FIGURE 2.3.** A group of women with their babies watching a demonstrator weigh an infant. Original caption: "Better Babies—A goal in demonstration work." L. C. Hanna, "Annual Report for Negro Women, State of Alabama, Year Ending Dec. 31, 1928." ACES Collection, box 356. Courtesy of Auburn University Libraries Special Collections and Archives.

**FIGURE 2.4.** Women sit on the porch of a new home. Original caption: "Mr. Will Dick's improved home in Macon County." L. C. Hanna, "Annual Report for Negro Women, State of Alabama, Year Ending Dec. 31, 1928." ACES Collection, box 356. Courtesy of Auburn University Libraries Special Collections and Archives.

FIGURE 2.5. Women, children, and a man are posed outside of a home, while another man in a suit looks on. Original caption: "Before—home of the Jarrett Family, Canaan Community, Montgomery County." L. C. Hanna, "Annual Report for Negro Women, State of Alabama, Year Ending Dec. 31, 1928." ACES Collection, box 356. Courtesy of Auburn University Libraries Special Collections and Archives.

FIGURE 2.6. Women and children chat on the front porch of a home while two men work on a new roof for the porch. Original caption: "After—Home of the Jarrett Family, Canaan Community, Montgomery County. Note old house in rear." L. C. Hanna, "Annual Report for Negro Women, State of Alabama, Year Ending Dec. 31, 1928." ACES Collection, box 356. Courtesy of Auburn University Libraries Special Collections and Archives.

FIGURE 2.7. Laura R. Daly talks with a family on their porch. Original caption: "The Agent talks it over with the Family—Montgomery County." L. C. Hanna, "Annual Report for Negro Women, State of Alabama, Year Ending Dec. 31, 1928." ACES Collection, box 356. Courtesy of Auburn University Libraries Special Collections and Archives.

decisions. Given that these photographs were taken by a professional photographer working for the USDA, with some of the photographs being featured in USDA official publications, they suggest that USDA officials approved of what agents like Hanna and Daly had devised—that is, practices designed to improve the living conditions of Black rural families. And indeed, analyses of annual extension reports and USDA publications reveal the truth of that suggestion. In the next section, I show why—even though the technologies and practices developed by Black home demonstration agents diverged from those sanctioned by federal guidelines—they were for the most part accepted by state and regional USDA leaders, and—up to a point—by local white landlords.

### "Dangerous to the Interest of the State"

Given the significance of cotton production to the economy of the U.S. South in the late nineteenth and early twentieth centuries, it's not surprising that concerns over the health and well-being of its labor force should be of paramount concern.[41] Furthermore, as many scholars have noted,[42] central to the culture of segregation and the maintenance of white supremacy was the belief that the Black population of the American South was inherently and bodily "problematic" and in need of improvement.[43] These dual concerns were articulated early and clearly by Robert S. Wilson, the head of Extension for the State of Mississippi, in the narrative summaries that he appended to his state's quantitative reporting forms that were sent each year to Washington, D.C. In a 1916 letter summarizing Black extension work that he wrote to Bradford Knapp, head of Extension for the South, Wilson begins by stating what the goal of that work is: "The object of Demonstration Work among the negroes is not only to increase the yielding capacity of their lands, and the earning capacity of the men, but there is a very great need of improvement and reform in their home life; especially are changes needed in the condition of their premises. Therefore, we have not thought best to load our negro agents down with regular demonstration farms, but rather to decrease, somewhat, the number of these demonstration plats, and give these agents more time for general work among their people."[44] Wilson is telling Knapp that he is in effect shifting the work of his Black male agents so that they can devote time and energy to the "improvement and reform" of their home life "among their people" instead of focusing solely on agricultural improvements. With few if any women agents in the state (1915 is just the beginning point for funded HDW), Wilson clearly felt strongly that African American home life was so problematic as to merit the re-assignment of work for his Black male agents. Near the end of the letter, and in a plea for additional funding, Wilson makes clear what the problem is:

> I wish to say that after observing results among negroes on a small scale, on which it has been conducted in Mississippi, I am fully convinced that we would be justified in a much larger expenditure for work among negroes. Mississippi is strictly an agricultural State, and a large majority of her laborers are negroes. Constituting, as they do, a tremendous asset to the State, or a tremendous burden, as the case may be, I think that it is imperative that we increase their efficiency in every possible way... they must be impressed with the importance of Sanitation and better care of their bodies; since it is a well known fact that, as a race, they are deteriorating physically, due to the unsanitary condition in their home and their immoral way of living.[45]

In other words, Wilson is concerned with the health of his laboring population, a population whose health is directly tied to the wealth of the state. And since for Wilson poor health was in fact brought on by "poor" behavior, those interventions were meant to improve both the physical conditions of home life, and also the moral/cultural "way of living." He concludes the report by asking for an additional $10,000 dollars "so that we may be able to employ a larger corps of negro workers whose duty it will be not only to instruct negroes as to better farming, but organize the young negroes into Corn and Pig Clubs, and to visit the homes of negroes and assist them in bringing about better home conditions."[46] In other words, Wilson's proposal for increased funding rested on his belief that teaching better farming techniques alone would not improve agricultural productivity; "immoral" workers would need to change their ways of living if they were to become a modern workforce.

Wilson reiterates these ideas in all of his reports throughout the 1910s and 1920s. In 1917, he made a direct plea to Washington for increased funding since, as he says, "the negroes compose such a large percent of our population, and such a large majority of our laboring population, it would be not only foolish, but dangerous to the interest of the state to undertake to keep them as ignorant and destitute."[47] And by 1917, the nature of those dangers to the interest of the state had become increasingly clear. The effects of what we today call the Great Migration—the movement of African American farmers from the U.S. rural South to cities and the North—were evident in most of the rural areas of the South, and Wilson must have been well aware of the declining rural labor force in his state.[48] It is within the context of a rapidly declining labor force, and the anxieties that this must have caused over cotton production and the wealth of the state, that Wilson and others begin to target Black home life. The entry of the United States into World War I in 1917 and the ensuing xenophobia caused a dramatic decrease in foreign immigration, further spurring African Americans to move North for industrial jobs.

In his reports, Wilson does his best to reassure Washington that his Black extension agents are working hard to maintain and retain the state's laboring population: "But it is not only in their work on the farm and with livestock that these negro agents are wielding a wholesome influence on the members of their race. They go into their homes, associate with them closely as the white agents cannot do and not only make suggestions but also assist them in bringing about more sanitary conditions at little expense. They also attempt constantly to impress upon these negroes the importance of clean living both physically and morally."[49] He also suggests why teaching rural women how to improve their homes and families by learning how to prepare more nutritious food and provide better clothing is particularly important: "The infant death rate among negro children, especially babies, has been very great and is yet greater than it should be. But great improvement is being brought about by the women being taught how, without extra expense, to more properly feed their children. And also how to make the most of materials they are able to secure in properly clothing themselves and their children."[50] Although he never addressed the issue of a labor shortage directly, Wilson is using the fear of such a shortage to legitimize his state's Black home extension work: improved living conditions, he is saying, would help alleviate this shortage directly by lowering mortality rates, and indirectly by providing fewer reasons for African Americans to leave the South. Not surprisingly, then, he supports the separate mission of Black home demonstration work: "These women carry on largely the same projects as the white women, except that sanitation and home improvement has been specially emphasized."[51]

Officials at the USDA offices in Washington, D.C., were aware of the labor situation in the rural South. W. B. Mercier, the assistant chief of the office of Extension in the South, dedicated a section of his pamphlet *Extension Work among Negroes 1920* to what he titled "Leaving the Farms," beginning with "A very serious problem during recent years in many farming sections had been the migration of Negro farmers to the towns and cities. This problem has affected the whites as well as Negroes to a considerable degree."[52] And like Wilson, Washington officials credited extension work with improving living conditions and thus retaining African Americans as the South's labor force. Oscar Martin, a high-ranking USDA official, pointed to land ownership and home improvement as keys to maintaining that labor, writing in 1924: "Home ownership is the largest factor in the solution of the so-called negro problem. Cooperative extension work, especially since the comprehensive organization of negro extension agents, has been one of the greatest influences in encouraging and helping negroes to become landowners and to succeed with land investments. In most parts of the Cotton Belt it has been possible during the last few years for farmers to make a good living and to make a profit besides. The migration to the North has perceptibly slackened."[53] In addition to enumerating the large number of women and girls engaged in gardening, food preparation, and preservation activities (as he notes, "12,355 women and 14,641 girls were enrolled in home gardening; 13,911 women and 13,826 girls, in food preservation; and 14,731 women and 16,537 girls, in food preparation"), and other work such as home improvement and beautification, Martin makes clear what he believes is the focus of the work: "Perhaps no phases of home demonstration work are more valuable among negroes than sanitation and health, which were exemplified by more than 10,000 negro homes."[54] For local and federal USDA officials, then, the loss of Black labor—either through migration or sickness— constituted a crisis that necessitated state interventions; and for local officials like Wilson, the dangers to the state involved not only the loss of productive capacity but also the fear of an unhealthy and possibly degenerate race interfering in the productivity of his state.

### Dangerous to the Race

The concerns about Black migration and the potential crisis of a scarcity of labor were shared by many members of the African American elites who believed in the discourse of racial uplift.[55] Thomas Campbell and other leaders at Tuskegee believed that little good could come of the northern migration of African Americans; instead they looked to improvements in living conditions in the rural South that could be brought about by helping farmers to help themselves. Summarizing her work for the year 1923, Black home demonstration agent for Tunica County, Mississippi, Julia Pegram addresses directly the issue of population loss: "Some contagion for the betterment of the Negro has undoubtedly swept thru Tunica County, for there has been more improvement in the living conditions than in any other phase of work touched by the efforts of the Extension Department. Though the exodus has struck this county the [improvement] from the ills seems to have in a measure replaced the shortage."[56] In other words, she suggests that an "improved" population provides almost as much labor as "more" population.

The leaders of Tuskegee Institute were so concerned about northern migration that they devoted their 1917 annual farmers conference to that theme. Newspaper clippings documenting the conference contain snippets of speeches and summaries of the primary addresses. The Buffalo, N.Y., *Courier's* opening paragraph provides a good overview of the conference themes:

> Declarations were adopted the most impressive of which constituted an appeal to both blacks and whites to check the emigration of the former to the north. To the south the negroes are acclimated, and their progress in land ownership and development has been accomplished. White labor being short in the north, they are tendered better wages than they have heretofore known, but the conference warns them that these conditions are transitory, whereas the south is believed to be entering upon its greatest era of development, and offers the colored people best and permanent opportunities.[57]

Tuskegee leaders believed that Black farmers needed to stay in the South and prove themselves worthy of equality through hard work in order to continue the economic and social progress they had made; northern migration might bring temporary gains, but the South remained the "best and permanent" option. And although Tuskegee leaders like Campbell were well aware of the multitude of reasons why many Black farmers were leaving the rural South, they rarely gave public voice to these concerns, and if they did the comments were so mild and indirect as to almost go undetected. In 1923, for example, Campbell wrote a note for the local white newspaper the *Montgomery Advertiser* chiding it and other white newspapers in the South for not providing any positive publicity about what he called the "new" southern "negro": "If the negro is needed to help develop this section . . . it is suggested that in their own way the daily white papers of the South carry on a system of publicity, setting forth some of the many good traits and virtues of the 'New' Southern Negro as a racial group." "Most of the Southern states," he argues, "are putting on advertising campaigns to attract white farmers from other sections into the South. Similar methods might be employed to help keep Negro labor here which the South already has."[58] His critique of the power of newspapers to create and reinforce racist stereotypes, in other words, was veiled as a suggestion, and one that would favor the white elites of the South by keeping "Negro labor here."

Of more immediate concern to Campbell and other USDA extension agents was the physical health of Black farmers. Unlike what Wilson and other white officials considered to be the cause of ill health of Black farmers—their "immorality"—Tuskegee leaders delineated the real causes of poor health—lack of sanitation, poor food, limited health care. And without pulling any punches, they made clear the costs that that poor health was causing the state. George Washington Carver, the now famous botanist working at Tuskegee as the head of the Department of Agriculture, spent much of his career developing nutritious food products that could be made from crops grown on southern soils such as peanuts and sweet potatoes.[59] Given his research into food and nutrition, he directed his attention to the health of Black farm laborers and particularly to diseases caused by malnutrition. As he wrote in 1917, "So, therefore, let us stop deceiving ourselves further, and strike at the very root of the trouble, which is poor food."[60] He then outlines succinctly the costs of ill health: "Careful statistics show that there are 112,000 Negro workers sick all the time, at an annual loss in earnings of $45,000,000; and that there are 450,000 seriously ill all the time, which means 18 days a year for each Negro inhabitant, at an annual cost of $75,000,000. It is also shown further that much of the sickness and 45 percent of all the deaths among Negroes are preventable."[61] Thomas Campbell echoed Carver's sentiments. He opens the section on home demonstration work in his 1923 annual report by arguing that the most important improvement during the year was the addition of a public health nurse who traveled extensively throughout the South teaching "practical sanitation among the people."[62] This was because, as he said, "one cannot work among the rural Negroes without being conscious of the fact that possibly the most neglected phase of public service among them is sanitation and health instruction." And the costs of such neglect could be catastrophic: "It is estimated by the Negro Year Book that ... the annual economic loss to the South from sickness and death among Negroes is probably $300,000,000 and that it would pay the South to spend alone, $100,000,000 to improve Negro health."[63] Campbell and Carver are certainly leaving no doubt about what was at stake concerning the ill health of Black farmers; for white landlords, the southern states, and the U.S. government, the economic costs were well beyond catastrophic. And for them—Campbell, Carver, other USDA Black officials, and Tuskegee leaders—the stakes were nothing less than the survival of their community.

Given these circumstances, it is not difficult to understand why Black home demonstration agents like Laura R. Daly and Luella Hanna focused their work on teaching women better methods of producing food, maintaining a clean home, and providing family health care. It was their way of walking the thin line between fulfilling the mandates put forward by USDA experts on home economics and meeting the actual needs of those women and their families whom they routinely encountered in their work. And because this shifting of federal dollars away from national mandates and toward the goal of improving Black farmers' lives did not disturb the workings of white supremacy in the Jim Crow South—and in fact supported it by maintaining a relatively healthy labor force at no cost to white landlords—the practices of Black home demonstration work were condoned by state, regional, and some federal USDA officials.

Of course, USDA Black home demonstration agents must have been aware that the improvements they brought to rural women were relatively insignificant compared to the racial and sexual oppression that Black women lived with daily, and their status as nonhumans within the structure of the Jim Crow South. Their work could provide material assistance to some women and their families, but left intact, at least for the moment, the various legal, economic, and social structures that constituted white supremacy. That was precisely the accommodation embedded in the ideology of racial uplift: small, gradual, material changes in the condition of Black lives would be tolerated if those changes occurred without threatening the status quo. But the goal of racial uplift as articulated by Washington and disseminated through the classrooms and hallways at Tuskegee was racial parity, a goal that did indeed threaten the systemic devaluing of Black lives that was necessary for plantation agriculture to succeed. Agents like Hanna and Daly, then, conducted their work to support Black farmwomen with a political intent. The material assistance they provided in terms of food production and health care was an important step toward home and land ownership and to eventual racial and economic justice. The gendered work of social reproduction was not simply the backdrop for the purportedly more important productive spheres of economic life, but in fact a necessary step toward liberation, a step that contained its own liberatory potential.[64] As Mullings has argued, the history of Black "life-work" in the Americas—that is, activities that sustain the health and well-being of Black lives and communities—from slavery onward reveals its role as a form of resistance. For enslaved peoples in the Caribbean, she maintains, "the importance of life-work . . . to resist the dispossession of their bodies and souls cannot be overstated."[65] The life-work of Black home demonstrators, in other words, was its own form of resistance.

Like her fellow agents, Laura Daly often used the narrative section of her annual reports—the section left open for the agent to mention other aspects of her work—to highlight her most important accomplishments. After enumerating the assistance she had provided in regard to sanitation, food production, and childcare in the first section of her forms, she would then describe in the narrative section how particular farm families had purchased and improved their homes and the role she had played in advising and supervising them. In her 1929 report, for example, she mentioned two new houses that were being constructed by Black farmers in Macon County but devoted much of her narrative to a complete description of a farmstead owned by Hill Taylor that was fully electrified and included indoor plumbing. The home, she wrote, "is a revelation to both white and colored folks who visit it daily. It shows what can be done even in the country, for many think that such conveniences as electric lights, hot and cold water, and bathroom facilities are to be had only in urban centers."[66] Taylor, in other words, had gained enough wealth to not only purchase his own farm but also to construct a home worthy of admiration by even white farmers. This was the meaning and the goal of Black home demonstration work: the sustaining of life and community, and resistance to dispossession in the form of independent, land-owning, Black farmers.

These narratives in the archive point to Daly's confidence in racial uplift; to her belief that her job as a home demonstrator would gradually show farm families how to produce enough food to sustain themselves and thrive so that they could purchase land and accrue capital. Daly's work, then, was also her politics, her way of gradually changing the position of Black farmers in the Jim Crow South so that they could be self-sustaining, and eventually landowners. Given the many constraints on Black consumerism, home demonstration agents focused on helping farm families sustain their health and acquire the goods they needed to maintain their economic independence on the land, not on what economists thought of as "rational" consumer behavior. This polite politics was not ushered in with fanfare but with restraint, and noticeable in the archive only by reading carefully the more open-ended sections of agents' monthly and annual reports. The archives leave little trace of a more direct resistance to plantation agriculture on the part of the USDA agents or the Black farmwomen they assisted, but one very powerful indication is found in the set of photographs included in Luella Hanna's 1928 report.[67] Figure 2.8 is a striking portrait of Mrs. Jamerson, a "club leader who can Can" as the original caption says. It is the only image within this set that features a Black woman as an individual subject. In other words, all of the other photographs in this set portray women and men as accessories to the work of home demonstration, either engaged in the work of demonstrating home skills as agents of the USDA or receiving such assistance. But in this photograph Mrs. Jamerson is neither assisting nor being assisted. Instead, she is motionless, with the focus on her gaze as she stares back at the camera. This image of an individual woman—of a person with ownership over their own subjectivity—constitutes a rare exception in the photographic archive of Black home demonstration work. Jamerson is depicted as proud, perhaps defiant, clearly strong, and most important, a full human being.[68] It is an exceptional image, made even more so by what it was working against: the norms through which Black USDA agents and the women they aimed to help negotiated their lives; norms that were impossible subject positions to fill.

And, given what I will discuss in the next chapter regarding the aesthetics of uplift, this representation of Jamerson becomes even more exceptional. As I document in chapter 3, one of the primary methods for delivering Black rural assistance had nothing to do with the USDA or the cooperative extension service. Rather, the movable school, as it came to be called, originated with Tuskegee's preeminent leaders: Booker T. Washington and George Washington Carver. It was a technology designed to deliver material assistance directly to poor Black farmers who had neither the time nor resources to attend lectures or demonstrations at Tuskegee. To legitimize its expense and highlight

**FIGURE 2.8.** Mrs. Jamerson posed in front of a display of canned goods. Original caption: "Mrs. Jamerson of Tyler Community, Dallas County. A Club Leader who can Can. She has 300 that look like this." L. C. Hanna, "Annual Report for Negro Women, State of Alabama, Year Ending Dec. 31, 1928." ACES Collection, box 356. Courtesy of Auburn University Libraries Special Collections and Archives.

its functionality, the literal and symbolic movement of the movable school was often represented verbally and visually in USDA documents. As I will discuss in the next chapter, with its constant movement through space (the rural areas of Alabama) and time (the "before" and "after" scenes of its accomplishment), the movable school could be presented as useful but nonthreatening, in stark distinction to the stasis of Mrs. Jamerson.

**CHAPTER 3**

# The Movable School and the Aesthetics of Uplift

In the spring of 1925, the British anthropologist Beatrice Blackwood visited Tuskegee Institute to collect data for her study of racial differences. She had asked the institute's president, Dr. Moton, for permission to observe Black children who attended school there and to measure, among other things, their head sizes, and he had reluctantly agreed. The USDA agents who were based at Tuskegee made sure that Blackwood did more than measure "difference"; they wanted her (like all visitors) to see what they were doing to alleviate "difference" in rural living conditions. In addition to her visits with Laura Daly to see the improvements that had been accomplished by the home demonstration agents, she was driven to a farm in Dallas County to spend a day observing the movable school. Her diary entries of that trip provide some of the most detailed descriptions of what was involved in the operations of the movable school.

She introduces the section with a description of how the school begins: "The truck fitted with supplies for teachings many practical things ... goes out to villages and stays a day in each place, all the people for miles round came, in cars and buggies, on horses and mules and foot." When she arrives at the actual farm, a group of men are digging a hole for an outhouse (and she comments "most of these houses have none") while women are learning how to make soap. During the day she watched demonstrations for women in "dressmaking, hat making, fireless cooking, preserving eggs, the selection of eggs for setting ... and talks on health and the care of babies." The demonstrations for "negro men" included "pruning and spraying peach trees, dealing with insect pests, how to plant and care for sweet potatoes and water melons." Late in the afternoon, she relates, Thomas Campbell delivered a speech to those gathered at the site stressing the importance of play and work, and then asking each guest to say a few words. The owner of the plantation—a Mr. Hardy—went on at length about how wonderful the movable school was since, in Blackwood's words, "no one had ever taught negroes what was the right and what was the wrong way of doing things" and that this was important given that "the prosperity of the South depended on both Negroes and Whites working together." Blackwood was then taken to the home of the plantation owner's daughter to have dinner and returned to the farm in the evening to watch—along with the school's participants—a short, documentary film made by the USDA that was meant to depict and legitimize the work done by its African American extension service. "Many of the audience had never seen a movie before" she continues, "and they laughed uproariously at everything, especially when they recognized Mr. Campbell."[1]

It is difficult to say for certain, of course, to what degree these events were staged for Blackwood and the other guests, and to what degree they reflect a normal day of work for the movable school, although according to the annual reports filed by Thomas Campbell and others that chronicle the activities of the USDA's African American extension service in Alabama, the activities Blackwood describes were fairly common. I open this chapter with Blackwood's visit because it provides a vivid and fairly accurate depiction of the movable school as it enacted the process of racial uplift and because it evokes the work that the movable school did not just for the farmers who were targeted, but for the various contingencies who used it as the centerpiece of the USDA's Tuskegee operations. Importantly, the movable school was a technology developed by and unique to the USDA's African American extension service. As such it was a great source of pride for Tuskegee-based USDA officials, and yet because it was not part of the larger USDA extension service its existence had to be continuously validated. As a result, and what I discuss in this chapter, Tuskegee's movable school became both the hallmark of Black extension work—one of its success stories—and a key publicity tool for local and regional USDA agents who needed to legitimize its expense to Washington, D.C. officials. The movable school was constantly being enacted and re-enacted, either to be witnessed personally and materially—like Blackwood did in 1925, and many other visitors who came to Tuskegee in the 1920s and 1930s—or discursively through verbal and visual depictions in reports, books, circulars, photographs, and film. What I document in this chapter is how these enactments of uplift—the movable schools' success stories—were used to justify the usefulness and cost of the movable school, thus ensuring that its work directly supporting poor Black farmers would continue. As long as the movable school was literally in motion throughout rural areas in Alabama and figuratively in motion as it transformed "before" scenes into "after" scenes, it presented no explicit threat to the status quo. And yet like home demonstration work, the movable school's successes at supporting poor Black farmers and sustaining Black life contained a future threat implied in the work of racial uplift.

Articulated most formally by Booker T. Washington, the discourse of uplift had broad appeal for Black and white elites in the late nineteenth and early twentieth centuries. Central to the discourse was the belief that with hard work and education African Americans could gradually work their way up the ladder to become respectable and modern Americans. This would require some help from white outsiders, but primarily would be actualized through self-help. These "respectable" African Americans would then become the teachers and leaders for the rest of the Black population as they too learned skills and moved into the middle class.[2] This is precisely what Blackwood was witnessing—African American leaders helping to uplift other members of their race. This chapter analyzes the various enactments of the movable school within the context of the discourse and aesthetics of uplift, and how those enactments left unnoted, or as in the USDA film that I will examine, quietly alluded to, the attainment of uplift's goal of racial justice. I show how the school both actualized and symbolized uplift through visual (film and photography) and verbal representations, and the ways in which different constituencies—Washington, D.C.-based USDA officials, Tuskegee-based USDA agents, and Campbell himself—mobilized that discourse for various uses. I first situate the movable school within the historical context of the USDA's extension service, highlighting its precarious position within the hierarchy of the agency, and the ways in which Tuskegee-based officials used the discourse of uplift to describe the school and legitimize its activities in their official reports. I then turn to a discussion of how the school became a form of uplift propaganda both for the USDA and for Tuskegee, each using the discourse of uplift but with different audiences in mind. I end the chapter with the ways in which the movable school and its uplift propaganda circulated beyond the United States and was referenced in accounts of British colonial governance in Africa. Throughout, I point to the accomplishments of the movable school in terms of improving Black lives, and how Tuskegee-based USDA agents were able to diminish the perceived threat of home and land ownership by always couching the movable school's accomplishments within the discourse of never-ending rounds of improvement; in other words, as never leading to racial justice.

## Legitimizing the Movable School

Beatrice Blackwood's description of her visit to the movable school was included in local agent Luella Hanna's 1925 official report of the activities of the school and was added to the State of Alabama's extension service's annual accounting to the federal government. Its inclusion, like the accounts of other visitors to Tuskegee, formed part of the official discourse that Tuskegee leaders deployed to legitimize the school's additional expense. When Blackwood visited Tuskegee, the apparatus of the movable school consisted of a truck that carried supplies and three USDA agents from the Black extension service: two women—a home demonstrator and a nurse—and a male farm demonstrator. But when the movable school was initially developed in the late nineteenth century it was simply a wagon carrying a few supplies. In his 1936 monograph *The Movable School Goes to the Negro Farmer*, Campbell traces the movable school to an initiative of Booker T. Washington who realized that few rural farmers could attend classes or conferences at Tuskegee and therefore that agricultural lessons were best taught through demonstrations and on the farms themselves.[3] George Washington Carver oversaw the construction of the first wagon—called the Jesup Wagon in honor of Morris K. Jesup, a New York philanthropist who had supplied funds for its construction.[4] When Thomas Campbell was hired as the first African American demonstration agent of the USDA in 1906, he took charge of the wagon, thus marking the entry of the movable school into the USDA's extension service. Campbell's annual government salary was $10; the bulk of his salary was paid for by Tuskegee and the General Education Board of the Rockefeller family philanthropy. The movable school, therefore, was not an initiative of the USDA's extension service, but rather was developed by Tuskegee leaders and was funded primarily through the institute and private philanthropic support.

In 1914, with additional and regularized funding made possible by the Smith-Lever Act, Tuskegee was able to add a home demonstrator agent to the school,[5] and in 1917 the wagon was replaced with a truck thus allowing access to more farming regions surrounding Tuskegee (fig. 3.1). It is in these years that what Blackwood describes as the movable school became a reality: the size and scope of its operations expanded and its position as a showpiece for Black extension work was established. Because the movable school did not fit into the organizational chart of the USDA's extension service and required funding for additional staff and equipment, its viability was almost always in question. The USDA field agent W. B. Mercier writing in 1920 about exten-

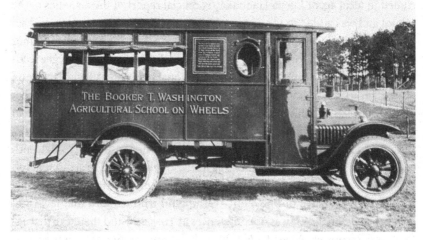

FIGURE 3.1. The movable school in 1917. Courtesy of the National Archives and Record Administration.

sion work for African Americans declares that in Alabama some effective extension work is being conducted through the movable school but concludes that "the expense in equipping and operating such an outfit is so great that it can not be recommended for general use."[6] It is useful, he argues, "for special uses in certain localities and under the management of a force having the personality and ability to impress the lesson."[7] Mercier is suggesting that if institutions like Tuskegee are willing to donate energy to overseeing the movable school's operations then it might be useful, but otherwise its emphasis on, as he says, "improving the house or the orchard," or benefitting "women and girls in some kind of home work"[8] is simply not worth the expense. But Campbell and other officials at Tuskegee thought otherwise and were continually writing in defense of the movable school.

Campbell's thirty-five page, 1920 memo outlining the history of Black extension work—a memo that was included in Alabama's annual report to the USDA—addresses the question of funding directly: "We are conscious of the fact that an auto truck does require a considerable outlay of funds for upkeep."[9] His fairly lengthy explanation of why those funds are justified is worth quoting here because it summarizes the primary reasons that Campbell and other Tuskegee-based USDA officials were keen promoters of the movable school:

> If our movable school force simply confined itself to the mere farmer's institute or lecture ideas of carrying on this project, I would be the first to recommend the discontinuance of it, but to the contrary, these workers using this truck, carry on the most practical and constructive kind of agriculture teaching, in a manner that is possibly more telling than any phase of extension teaching ever instituted for the uneducated country people, in conjunction, of course, with the local agents on the grounds, without whom we could not do our best work. Educators, Social Settlement, Red Cross and other public workers from all over the country have been attracted by this form of rural work and are frequently calling for the Alabama plan, with the idea of adopting some such system in connection with their work. I am tempted to say that movable school work is more adaptable to Negroes than to whites, for the simple reason that it reaches "the man farthest down" who lives in the most remote sections of the rural districts and the methods used by our workers must necessarily be elementary, so as to instruct this class of people. To this end, an effort is made by all local agents, where a movable school had been held in their territory, to use these demonstrations as the beginning of a definite and systematic method of teaching better farming and more comfortable home surroundings.[10]

First, as Campbell makes clear, the movable school provides services that differed from other forms of agricultural extension—services that are "the most practical and constructive" and that serve as the "beginning of a definite and systematic method of teaching better farming and more comfortable home surroundings." Second, the movable school is important because it is "more adaptable to Negroes than to whites" as it uses "elementary" methods of instruction that are required to reach "the man farthest down." And third, the movable school serves as a model for "educators, social settlement, Red Cross and other public workers from all over the country" who presumably are also hoping to reach a certain "class of people" and apply the "Alabama plan" to social reform efforts. The movable school was important, Campbell suggests, because it was a distinctive technology for supporting Black farm families, teaching basic skills to the most remote and impoverished farmers who otherwise would be out of the reach of the USDA's extension service. As an enactment of uplift, he suggests, it serves as a model of rural reform efforts.

Given the need for on-going financial support, it is not surprising that Campbell and Tuskegee officials built discursively and materially on the notion of the distinctiveness of the movable school as a model of self-help and liberal development for the poorest farmers. In the same year as Campbell's and Mercier's reports, Henry Simms and Juanita Coleman—Black USDA agents who worked with the movable school—authored a USDA official circular describing the accomplishments of the movable school.[11] Their visual and verbal descriptions provide clear evidence of how the school enacted uplift. Figures 3.2 and 3.3, for example, provide visual proof of the effectiveness of the movable school in improving farm homes, as they depict what the labor of Black farmers under the guidance of the USDA can accomplish: a whitewashed and repaired house with new fencing. Similarly, other before and after images portray the labor required for the construction of a new poultry house. In the preface to the circular, Campbell carefully outlines the goals of the movable school while assuring white plantation owners that these accomplishments work to their favor. "The real object" of the school, he writes, is to provide "concrete illustrations" to Black farmers "proving that they can do better work, make more produce, on a smaller number of acres of land, at less expense, and at the same time beautify their homes." This work, he continues, only proceeds after USDA agents secure permission "from the white landlord . . . to make a model of one or more houses on each plantation at negligible cost, for these simple and practical demonstrations go far towards stimulating the interest of the Negro farmer in his home and strengthening his attachment for it, even though he does not own it."[12] In other words, Campbell is assuring white landlords that the "simple and practical" improvements brought by the movable school do not in any way threaten the social order; instead they promote "the interest" of Black tenants in caring for their homes.

This balance between promoting the accomplishments of the movable school on the one hand and on the other suggesting that the support the school was providing to poor Black farmers did not threaten white landlords became a characteristic discursive strategy of Campbell and his peers. Throughout the 1920s, most of the annual reports sent to Washington, D.C. describing the achievements of the African American extension service in Alabama included an addendum specifically on the work of the movable school. Luella Hanna's 1925 report is filled with detailed accounts of the daily activities of the movable school. In one such account, Hanna relates what happens when the white plantation owner and his wife come to "inspect" the accomplishments of the movable school at the end of a day's labor. After examining the new steps into the farmhouse, the fireless cooker, and a hat that had been made, Hanna quotes the wife as saying, "I did not believe that these things could be made so simple; it is all just fine and wonderful. We are all going to live here, and we want you to have everything, just as comfortable as we can

**FIGURE 3.2.** Before the movable school came. Harry Simms and Juanita Coleman, "Movable Schools of Agriculture among Negroes in Alabama," Circular 39, Auburn: Alabama Polytechnic Institute Extension Service, 1920, p. 20. Courtesy of Auburn University Libraries Special Collections and Archives.

**FIGURE 3.3.** After the movable school came. Harry Simms and Juanita Coleman, "Movable Schools of Agriculture Among Negroes in Alabama," Circular 39, Auburn: Alabama Polytechnic Institute Extension Service, 1920, p. 21. Courtesy of Auburn University Libraries Special Collections and Archives.

make it. We are going to help you make these improvements because they will benefit us as well as they will you."[13] The point that Hanna is trying to make is obvious: the uplift that is being accomplished by the movable school—with the "help" of white landowners—presents no threat to them or to white supremacy. Blackwood's description of her visit to the movable school reinforces the point. She ends her summary with a sentiment similar to the plantation owner's wife: "In such work as this lies the hope of better living conditions for the Southern Negroes, and so of better days for the community as a whole, for, in some districts at least, the Negroes out-number the whites ten to one, and it is clear, therefore, that the prosperity of the Negroes is just to that extent an index of the prosperity of the South." For Blackwood, the movable school was a win-win; it improved tenant farmers' lives and livelihoods, thereby providing white plantation owners with a healthier labor force at little or no expense to them. The movable school indeed was bringing "better days for the community as a whole."[14] Tuskegee-based USDA officials, then, materially and discursively represented the movable school as an enactment of uplift that was on-going, always framing its accomplishments as beneficial to Black tenant farmers *and* their white landlords.

## The Movable School as Uplift Propaganda

HELPING NEGROES TO BECOME BETTER FARMERS AND HOMEMAKERS

When Beatrice Blackwood visited Tuskegee in 1925 and described her day at the Hardy Plantation, the film shown to the community in the evening that elicited such laughter from the audience when they recognized Thomas Campbell was titled *Helping Negroes to Become Better Farmers and Homemakers*. Produced in 1921 by the USDA, it was the first of several such films meant to promote the work of the USDA's African American extension service, focusing particularly on what the USDA was doing to stem the migration of Black labor out of the South. Similar to other divisions of the USDA, the motion picture section was meant to produce material that could be used both as educational documents for extension work and to showcase the extension service's many accomplishments.[15] The movable school features prominently in the film, with documentation of one day's work at the farmhouse of the Collins family comprising more than half of its twenty-minute length. The film provides important insights into how Washington, D.C.-based USDA officials hoped to educate Black farmers, and how they represented and legitimized the movable school for a much wider audience, including white plantation owners.

As historian J. Emmett Winn has argued, from the opening credits through to the end the film is filled with racist stereotypes, portraying African Americans as "pickanannies" and "jesters."[16] In addition, it depicts white USDA agents and officials as the key actors in the transformation of the Collins house and more generally in regard to the work of the USDA Black extension service. As Winn notes, not only is this incorrect (white agents rarely attended a movable school, nor were they the ones who developed it), it totally ignores the work done by Tuskegee officials, Campbell, and the staff of the USDA African American extension service, in addition to the community members who actualized the movable school. In this way, the USDA was presenting Black extension work within a vernacular that not only did not threaten, but in fact reinforced, white supremacy. Yet Campbell and his peers at Tuskegee found the film useful for their educational efforts, and it was shown repeatedly to Black farmers they were trying to assist.[17] In this section, I analyze the film's visual and verbal depictions of Black extension work and show how the film promoted and reinforced the ideology of racial uplift in terms of its ongoing enactments, while only hinting at the politics implied in those enactments.

My analysis draws on the work of Allyson Nadia Field who demonstrates in her book *Uplift Cinema* how the accommodationist beliefs of Booker T. Washington and others were visualized and communicated through what she calls "uplift aesthetics."[18] Developed partly to persuade northern philanthropists to support Hampton and Tuskegee Institutes and partly to provide concrete, visual exemplars of uplift for African Americans, uplift aesthetics characterized an entire genre of late nineteenth and early twentieth centuries fictional accounts, films, pageants, promotional brochures, and visual images. According to Field, two tropes are key indicators of uplift aesthetics: visual displays of labor and images that depict "before" and "after" scenes of improvement. Visual displays of labor make clear that uplift is only gained through hard work and self-improvement, while before and after scenes of improvement provide visual evidence of the accomplishments of uplift (the after scenes), but also reminders of a potential slip backward if the hard work of uplift is not continued (the before scenes). Both of these characteristics of uplift aesthetics are evident in *Helping Negroes to Become Better Farmers and Homemakers*. The film begins by introducing the Collins family, all depicted individually and collectively at work. The husband Rube Collins is shown working at his anvil, his wife Hannah is collecting water from the well, their son Obe is practicing his shooting skills, and daughter Ca'line is feeding the chickens. The following scene portrays the whole family including other unnamed children working in the cotton fields. Thus, the family is portrayed as hard working and therefore worthy of the assistance that the USDA is providing. These visual displays of labor are continuous throughout the film; only at the end, after the movable school has completed its work, is the family shown in repose.

The narrative arc that holds the story together is the process of improvement brought by the USDA as staged through a time sequence of two years, from the opening when Rube Collins recognizes the pest in his cotton field, a recognition that precipitates interventions, to the closing when the entire family gathers on the remodeled front porch and gathers around the phonograph. The film stages that improvement process in two parts. First, white USDA agents are brought in to offer advice on how to cultivate and harvest cotton to minimize the threat of a boll weevil infestation and to provide lessons on how to diversify the family's crops to reduce their reliance on cotton. These strategies were central to the USDA's boll weevil national eradication programs.[19] The second part of the improvement process depicted in the film is the movable school, and as discussed earlier, this intervention was not nationwide, but was particular to the Black extension service.

The film opens and closes at the Collins farm home that serves as the key site of the USDA improvements. That site is comprised of two separate cabins, one that is built from logs and one that is timbered. Both cabins appear to be in disrepair, without proper doors or windows. The film portrays a neighbor alerting Rube Collins that boll weevils have been discovered in their fields. After consulting with his landlord and later with white USDA agents, Collins apparently adopted the recommended reforms in cultivating and harvesting cotton as the caption reveals what has transpired: "Two years later, better farming has given the Collins family a better home, and a local negro agent to assist the white county agent has become necessary." That "better home" is significantly different from the two cabins in disrepair; in fact, it appears to be a completely new home. The home has proper sash windows, two chimneys, and its exterior is finished with board and batten siding. This provides clear visual evidence of the success that resulted from taking the advice of white USDA agents. Yet as the caption suggests, that success is just one stage of a process; now, a "negro agent has become necessary." Because the film was made by the USDA to validate its extension services—both white and Black—the film makes clear that both divisions are necessary: white agents are needed to dispense scientific advice on farming, advice that can help African American farmers but that can only go so far in intervening in their lives; while Black agents are necessary because they can get closer, literally, to Black bodies. As the film progresses, it becomes clear that the new home is simply one stage in the process of improvement.

The rest of the film is dedicated to depicting how Black agents working with the movable school complete the modernization of the house and farm. In the opening sequence of this section, men are shown whitewashing the outside of the house, and then quite abruptly the old stairs leading to the entrance are removed while a new stoop and stairway are brought in. The old poultry house is removed and a new one constructed, the crumbling outhouse is replaced, and shrubs and ornamental plants are planted in front of the house. The camera then moves between groups of people working on various home projects, staged in ways that point to the USDA agent's role in improving farmers' home life. At one point the camera focuses on a USDA agent demonstrating how to build a poultry house, while in another the focus is on a home demonstration agent teaching the best way to use a fireless cooker. After the movable school truck leaves, the caption states, "Thus Collins and his neighbors learn how to improve their homes." The camera pans the house façade, newly whitewashed and landscaped with Hannah sitting on the front porch and moves to the right to include the new poultry house. The final caption presents surprising information: "So Rube Collins becomes a contented farm owner; thankful for the prosperity extension work has helped to bring him." How exactly Collins is able to buy his farm and home through the two-year timeframe that the film encapsulates is left entirely unclear. Presumably, the assumption is that through hard work, and with the help of both Black and white USDA agents, the Collins family had saved enough money to make this important purchase. The last scene in the film highlights what farm ownership has brought to the Collins family. They are depicted sitting on the new front steps of their shiny, white home listening to a phonograph brought by some guests. Here they are posed in clean and formal clothing, the women in white dresses, the men with ties. They are the proper heteropatriarchal family, entertaining guests with modern cultural accouterments such as the phonograph.

The film's use of before and after shots, and the ongoing staging of Black labor and self-help clearly accord with what Field has called the "visual aesthetics of uplift." The Collins family has been uplifted through their own labor, but also with the assistance of white USDA extension agents who have brought improvements to the Collin's family farm and Black agents who have brought improvements to the Collins family home. White and Black sections of the USDA's extension service are shown to be distinct and separate, with white agents who initiate and oversee the process. But the fact that the film ends with the transformation of Rube Collins from a tenant farmer to a farm owner reveals one of the key contradictions embedded in USDA's improvement strategies for southern farming. Transforming tenant farmers into farm owners was one of the most important objectives of the USDA's extension service, as northern agricultural experts had identified sharecropping and tenancy as problems particular to the U.S. South that were impeding rural improvement and agricultural modernization.[20] Land ownership was also a key indicator of uplift as defined by Washington and as practiced through the Agricultural Departments at Hampton and Tuskegee and through the USDA's African American extension service. But assisting Black farmers to free themselves from the ties of indebtedness that held them in place as tenant farmers and sharecroppers was certainly not in the interests of white landowners, and promotion of that goal was a direct threat to plantation-style cotton production. The film unquestionably downplays this objective; without any visual attention given to it, a viewer might easily overlook the fact that Collins had become a farm owner. In addition, the overt racist depictions of African Americans that are littered throughout the film must have assured white plantation owners that the work of the movable school and the USDA's Black extension service presented no real threat to the racial order of Jim Crow. And yet the fact that the film ends with an image of Black land ownership indicates its importance as the end goal of uplift and the ultimate achievement of the work of the movable school. Thus, the film incorporates different messages to different audiences, negotiating between USDA federal mandates, Black farmers and extension workers, and local white landlords.

A similar set of negotiations is evident in the film's depictions of sport and recreation. As discussed in chapter 2, anxieties over the poor health of Black farmers were shared by plantations owners, Tuskegee leaders, and USDA officials, and therefore a good deal of the USDA's initiatives focused on improving the physical health of Black farmers. Most contemporary descriptions of the activities of the movable school mention sporting and recreational events as important components of the school, in addition to lessons about health and childcare. The film devotes several minutes to depictions of these events, focusing on a girls' volleyball game and foot races for boys. As Gabriel Rosenberg has documented, attention to physical fitness was a key element of 4-H—the division of the USDA's extension service aimed at children—as it was meant to create "wholesome" girls and boys and shape a future, modern, citizenry.[21] Yet, as many scholars have shown, the idea and the image of Black, particularly male, athletic bodies posed a deep-seated threat to white patriarchy, and formed the linchpin of white terror campaigns.[22] The film counters this threat with the use of overt racist stereotypes and comedic staging. The winners of the girls' volleyball game are awarded, according to the caption, the "fruits of victory"—watermelon—and the film stages the event as if it was a messy, childlike competition, in accord with racist stereotypes, while the film's depiction of the men's "shoe" race downplays any threats by presenting it as humorous, with the players scrambling for the correct shoes and winners seemingly arbitrarily chosen, while ending with the treat of watermelon. In this way, the practices devised by the USDA's African American extension service to improve the health of Black farmers were presented to white audiences as nothing more than entertainment—literally games—that were in no way threatening to white supremacy.

As Blackwood's opening description suggests, Black audiences also viewed this film. According to Campbell, a movie projector with accompanying

USDA films became part of the regular "technologies" carried by the movable school in the early 1920s. In 1925, when Blackwood visited, the film she watches must have been *Helping Negroes to Become Better Farmers and Homemakers* as it was the only film at that point produced by the USDA that described African American extension work. "Many . . . had never seen a movie before" she writes, and "they laughed uproariously at everything, especially when they recognized Mr. Campbell." So clearly the film was a form of entertainment for them as well as an educational tool. The act of recognizing Campbell—that someone whom they knew was featured in what was this new mechanized form of entertainment—sparked the most laughter, but their continuous laughter points to other comedic aspects as well: to the novelty of seeing a moving image, of seeing people like themselves depicted in it, and of seeing the intentionally humorous racist depictions. Blackwood does not discuss her own reaction to the film, nor does she mention what must have been Black spectators' feelings of unease and anger elicited by the film's overt racism. Most likely she did not notice its racist stereotypes. In her diary entries she often takes umbrage at the unfair treatment of and violence aimed at African Americans, yet the very reason she was visiting Tuskegee—to measure physical differences between Blacks and whites as part of the "scientific" study of racial difference—points to her own deep-seated racist views, views that were widely held by liberal elites in the United States and United Kingdom. She would not have seen the contradiction between advocating for fair legal treatment for African Americans, while believing in their essential difference. In a similar way, the film serves as a promotional tool for the USDA's work improving the lives of Black farmers, yet within a context in which those farmers are depicted as essentially different from and less than white farmers. The film portrayed the movable school as a key technology of uplift, but—in the hands of the Washington, D.C.-based USDA officials—those depictions of uplift were framed to minimize, though not extinguish, their potential threat to white power.

### THE MOVABLE SCHOOL GOES TO THE NEGRO FARMER

In a way similar to *Helping Negroes to Become Better Farmers and Homemakers*, Campbell's 1936 book, *The Movable School Goes to the Negro Farmer*, provides testaments to the efficacy of the movable school as a successful strategy of rural improvement, one that would potentially transform Black tenant farmers into landowning, prosperous citizens. Yet unlike the film, Campbell's book is not laced with racist stereotypes, nor does it disguise the potential ways that this transformation could lead to significant changes to the plantation system.

Nonetheless, Campbell does his best to highlight that uplift is a long-term process of change, not a radical challenge to the system. The book is a curious mixture of genres, part autobiography, part history of Tuskegee and the USDA's African American extension service, and part first-person testimonials to the success of the movable school. Published in the heart of the Great Depression—a time when Campbell and others at Tuskegee were acutely aware of the impoverished conditions of tenant farmers and sharecroppers living in the rural South—the book provides three related but separate stories of uplift and development that deploy what Field has called a "rhetorical strategy of uplift."

The first story is what Campbell calls his "semi-autobiography" comprising the first three chapters of the book: Childhood and Early Struggles, The Trip to Tuskegee, and Tuskegee at Last. The titles of those chapters are fairly telling as Campbell begins by relating stories of the struggles of his family while growing up in rural Georgia with a father who was a tenant farmer left to raise six children on his own after the death of his mother. His older siblings were sent to work to pay off debts, leaving him and his younger sister alone without care or food. Campbell narrates the details of how he made the trip from Georgia to Tuskegee in chapter 2—a trip that took him more than three months to complete—through a series of what he calls five "deceptions." His escape from home in the early hours of January 2, 1899, was his first deception—his father had forbidden him to go. These deceptions—or obstacles—continue along the journey as he is forced to find work, often lying about his intentions, until finally with deception number five (Campbell cleverly found a way to get a ride near to Tuskegee without paying for it) he arrived at the school on April 26, 1899. The redemption that might be implied by the title of chapter 3—"Tuskegee at Last"—is not immediately actualized in Campbell's narration of his schooling at Tuskegee, a narration that includes continuous struggles to find resources and to sort out what vocation he will pursue. Only in the last several pages does he write of his dedication to rural life and agriculture, ending with the apparently surprising news that in the fall of 1906, after returning to Tuskegee to begin graduate work, he was appointed the first African American extension worker: "At the close of the second's summer's work I returned to the Institute to pursue graduate study. I had just begun my advanced study when Dr. Washington recommended me to the Federal Government to be the first to hold the position of Negro Extension Agent."[23] Thus Campbell's semi-autobiography, like Washington's *Up From Slavery*, is a story of personal uplift and redemption: his extremely humble and impoverished roots, his journey to better himself through education and hard work (but still corrupted by his necessary but spiritually bankrupt deceptions), and his eventual appointment as the first African American hired by the U.S. government to help uplift other African Americans, thus redeeming his sins.

Campbell narrates the history of the movable school in the second section of the book, from Booker T. Washington's early recognition of the limited reach of Tuskegee's educational facilities to the purchase of the large truck in 1923 that allowed the school to reach remote farmers quite a distance from Tuskegee. Inserted quite liberally throughout the narrative are lengthy quotes presumably taken from contemporary reports and letters describing the actions of the movable school at particular places and times, thus adding authenticity to Campbell's assertions of its many successes. As with all official accounts of the movable school, Campbell takes care to point out that key to its success is teaching Black farmers how to help themselves; that is, with minimal expenditure but with a lot of hard work, Black farmers can bring themselves out of poverty, just as Campbell's semi-autobiography as related in the first part of the book had demonstrated.

This historical accounting of the movable school is accompanied by a series of before and after photographs, one literally captioned as such. The opening image is comprised of two photographs that allude to the past (or the "before") but are contemporary images (fig. 3.4). The bottom image titled "The Old Settler" depicts an elderly woman sitting on the porch of (presumably) her house. The caption reveals her status as a daughter of ex-slaves who was visited by Washington on his early trips through Macon County; trips during which Washington initiated the idea of a movable school. Thus, she bears witness to that past and to some of the early accomplishments of the school, as she is photographed making a basket, having learned how to "work with [her] hands." But it's clear from the image that the process of uplift is far from completed: she is barefoot and is dressed in clothing reminiscent of the mid-nineteenth century, and the house is in rough shape with the porch floorboards rotting away and the exterior wallboards barely holding together. The caption of the top photograph resumes the narrative by suggesting that what was true of the past—poor housing—continues into the present. The most striking feature of this image is the fence that is seemingly in disrepair; it's constructed of different size planks held together loosely, some of which seem to be rotting. The focus of the image is the gate that appears to be falling apart both on the left and right sides. The house itself is not obviously in disrepair, though the external chimney is patched with an array of materials and is not standing at ninety degrees. Unlike the "old settler" the two "rural youth" are standing and looking at the camera thus depicting them with some agency, presumably to be put into action with a visit of the movable school. Thus,

**FIGURE 3.4.** A woman weaving a basket in front of a run-down home (*bottom*); two children posed in front of a house with a dilapidated fence (*top*). Thomas Monroe Campbell, *The Movable School Goes to The Negro Farmer*, Tuskegee, Ala.: Tuskegee University Press, 1936, between pp. 77 and 79.

The Rural Negro Youth and the Home in Which He Lives Still Constitutes a Serious Problem

One of the Few Old Settlers Who Remembers When Booker T. Washington Came to Macon County and Began Teaching the Children of Ex-Slaves How to Work with Their Hands

the two images combine past and present to show what work has been done by the movable school and to suggest what is left to do, thereby also hinting at the future. The girl in the foreground is, like the older woman, barefoot—presumably she has not yet been taught about hookworm—but as youth, both she and the boy represent the future with the chance that their "serious problems" can be fixed by the movable school.

The second set of images is explicitly labeled as "before and after" photographs of an outdoor toilet (fig. 3.5). The juxtaposition of the two images makes clear the "progress" being made by the staff of the movable school, as a poorly built outhouse is replaced by a new, well-constructed outhouse. It does not require any deep visual reading skills to understand which of the two images depicts before; the rough framing, irregular and off-kilter boards, and the seemingly haphazard privacy cloth of the top image give it away immediately. That the interior is not even shown but instead is blackened suggests its condi-

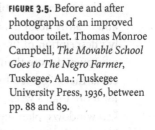

FIGURE 3.5. Before and after photographs of an improved outdoor toilet. Thomas Monroe Campbell, *The Movable School Goes to The Negro Farmer*, Tuskegee, Ala.: Tuskegee University Press, 1936, between pp. 88 and 89.

A Before and After Demonstration in Home Sanitation for the Family Unit

tion is so unsanitary that it can't be represented to the public. The bottom image by contrast depicts the clean and orderly interior of the outhouse, newly constructed with a proper roof, walls and doorway, and denotes the process through which the new outhouse was built. Presumably the movable school—represented here by the man with the suit—has visited the farm and used communal labor to complete the construction. The three figures are posed in such a way as to suggest that the Tuskegee man is pointing out to the occupants of the farm the sturdiness of the toilet construction. Thus, the viewer is watching an uplifted African American teach other African Americans how to be modern and uplift themselves, a key trope of the aesthetics of uplift.

The final section of Campbell's book—titled "Exemplary Achievements"—describes the tangible results of the movable school by explaining how the material benefits it brought to Black farm families were themselves part of the process of uplift. In other words, it provides evidence of how improvements made by the movable school became models for the community. From the descriptions of the three sites that Campbell chooses, it is clear that the models created by the movable school were not simply modern farms, but modern and healthy homes. The first site was the farm of Hill Taylor (for Laura Daly's description of the farm, see chapter 2), a relatively affluent Black farmer who owned more than five hundred acres of land. Campbell describes how local farmers, "guided by the movable school force," worked on the farmhouse for more than a week, refurbishing the inside, repairing fences, replacing broken windows, planting a flower garden, in order to make "a striking contrast between the 'improved' and 'unimproved.'"[24] According to Campbell, the Hill Taylor project then served as a model for other farm families in nearby communities who wanted to improve their homes and he provides "first-hand" accounts from three different people who discuss how they were inspired by visiting the farm. Each of these first-person accounts follows the uplift narrative, all starting with their early impoverished lives and ending with the staff of the movable school helping them design and construct new homes. Mary Simpson of Macon County, for example, relates the many financial and personal hardships of her early life, but following "the advice of Booker T. Washington" she is able to succeed at diversified farming, and when her house burned down and her neighbors encouraged her to buy a car with the insurance money, she instead "got in touch with Mrs. L. R. Daly, my home demonstration agent, because I knew of how she had helped to improve the Hill Taylor place in another community."[25] Tom Moss relates how he initially adopted poor farming techniques but with help from the local USDA agent his farm and its outputs increased. After seeing the Hill Taylor house, he and his wife decided to improve their own home, and later constructed a new house using the advice of the movable school staff whom he had to call "again and again for their helpful ideas and advice."[26] Similarly, O. C. Crowe of Montgomery County tells the story of how, inspired by the words of Washington, he was able to get out of tenancy and buy the small farm that he gradually is able to enlarge. He and his wife were taken by the farm and home demonstration agents to see the Taylor project, and they used their assistance to remodel the home and add a modern bathroom.

Each of these projects is accompanied by an illustration comprised of several photographs, illustrations that make clear what Campbell means by "exemplary achievements." The Hill Taylor illustration takes the form of the "before and after," with the two photographs on the left depicting the "after" and the two on the right the "before" (fig. 3.6). The signs of uplift are visually evi-

The Hill Taylor and Similar Projects Have Inspired Many Families to Take Their First Step Towards Home Improvement
Top and Bottom Left: After the Movable School
Top and Bottom Right: Before the Movable School Came
Center: A Terracing Demonstration

FIGURE 3.6. Before and after photographs of Hill Taylor's farm. Thomas Monroe Campbell, *The Movable School Goes to The Negro Farmer*, Tuskegee, Ala.: Tuskegee University Press, 1936, between pp. 136 and 137.

dent. In the top images note that the rickety fence has been removed, glass windows have been replaced, the front yard has been tidied and a walkway added, the porch has been cleared and a bench added, and the tree and shed in front of the house have been removed. The comparison of the bottom two images is difficult since the photos are not taken from the same position, but one can notice that the after image does not feature the rickety fence or outbuilding. As Campbell writes, "Guided by the Movable School force, the visiting farmers and their families worked wonders at this home during the week."[27] There is no textual reference to farm improvements, but the figure includes a photograph depicting the movable school's agricultural mission; in this case the caption tells us that the photograph depicts a terracing demonstration. As Campbell writes, the Taylor project was meant to serve as a "laboratory"[28] and an "example"[29] of home improvement. The photographs of the Mary Simpson-Carliss project show a modern bungalow house with indoor plumb-

**64** Chapter Three

**FIGURE 3.7.** Photographs showing Tom Moss's old and new home. Thomas Monroe Campbell, *The Movable School Goes to The Negro Farmer*, Tuskegee, Ala.: Tuskegee University Press, 1936, between pp. 140 and 141.

ing, a modern kitchen, and separate living and dining rooms. This set of photographs is notable for the absence of any before images, yet the textual references to Mary Simpson's life story make clear what her earlier house looked like, and the caption—this house "commands the respect and admiration of the people in her community"[30]—alludes to the future in the form of assumed transformations in the community.

That the movable school was far less about teaching modern farming techniques as it was about giving lessons in what Higginbottom calls "respectability politics" is made explicit in the set of three photographs that illustrate the

Tom Moss project (fig. 3.7).[31] The center and bottom photograph depict Moss's old house and new house; like Mary Simpson, the exemplary achievement of the movable school was not a transformation of a house but the construction of an entirely new home. And that the house is now a home is illustrated by the top photograph, depicting, presumably, Tom Moss, his wife, and three children. The setting and layout of the photograph suggest the quintessential patriarchal, heteronormative, middle-class family. The family members are posed in the living room busily improving themselves in gender-normative ways: two boys are playing with blocks on the floor, the daughter is looking on as her mother, seated in a rocking chair, reads a book. The mother and daughter pair create a prototypical image of proper femininity—a mother leaning back in her rocking chair (a sign of maternal deference) sharing with her daughter the emblem of civilization—a book.[32] The father sits apart in his own space on a larger chair reading a magazine. The propriety of the family is further established by the home furnishings: a fireplace and mantel, proper window and window coverings, a light fixture indicating electricity, and carpets—all signs of a modern American home. Similar to the final scene of *Helping Negroes Become Better Farmers and Homemakers*, this posed image suggests the ultimate goal of uplift: an educated, modern, patriarchal, heteronormative, land-owning farm family. The section ends with Campbell mentioning how the movable school has become an object of study by foreign visitors including "educators, social workers, Red Cross and public workers who see in [the movable school] wonderful possibilities for developing backward peoples."[33]

Thus in style and content *The Movable School Goes to the Negro Farmer* relates stories of transformation and uplift: Campbell's personal story of uplift actualized through hard labor as related in his semi-autobiography; the story of the origins, development, and eventual success of the movable school; and the story of the promised future brought about by the movable school, a story of the uplift of the "rural Negro people to the established American standard of living."[34] Both the movable school, and Campbell's book about it, provided proof of the power of racial uplift and the concrete ways that the USDA's African American extension service was supporting Black farmers. And like the film *Helping Negroes Become Better Farmers and Homemakers* Campbell's book focuses on the hard work needed to distinguish the "before" from the "after," an "after" that included home and land ownership.

### From Uplift to Development

As I've shown, almost from its inception, the movable school was used by Tuskegee officials and later the USDA to showcase their accomplishments with rural Black farmers. By all accounts, foreign visitors to Tuskegee like Beatrice Blackwood were encouraged to spend time at local sites where movable schools were being conducted. Campbell and other agents of the USDA's Black extension service highlighted the visits of foreigners in their annual reports to Washington, D.C., and in other public venues like newspaper accounts, often including letters or quotes from the letters of these visitors. For example, in the 1921 annual report of the movable school three sets of foreign visitors were mentioned: "Mr. and Mrs. Wilkie, missionaries from Gold Coast West Africa, Mr. and Mrs. Winger, missionaries from Central Africa, Mr. and Mrs. Omen, missionaries from West Africa."[35] "Native Africans are coming into the south to study the best methods of agriculture and to carry the information back to their people," Campbell is quoted as saying in the newspaper the *Montgomery Advertiser* in 1924, and he goes on to quote from a letter written by K. W. G. Donma of Liberia: "The school on wheels is especially noteworthy, not alone on account of its uniqueness, but for its great work as well. Thousands yearly are affected directly or indirectly by this school. Their own condition is not only bettered, but they in turn, influence others. This is not only a local or national work, but is world-wide, as students and missionaries from other countries come here to catch the vision of how things are done, that they may carry the work on in other lands."[36]

Campbell's 1925 annual report included commentary from a Father Harry Buck of the Saint Augustine Mission in Southern Rhodesia, who praises the work of Tuskegee in general and of the movable school in particular: "To see one at work was inspiration, and the value of the concentrated efforts of the demonstrators, the trained nurse and the home economics teacher and the extension workers, giving such simple and practical and such obviously useful instructions, in a community, cannot be estimated. It must gradually lift the whole race, man and women, boys and girls, and that is a Christian work to do. We could only long for the day when the tiny beginnings just made in vast Africa by a mere handful of farm demonstrators should spread everywhere, and be as effective, as happy and as helpful as that which one has been privileged to see in this country."[37] And in his 1928 report Campbell included transcriptions of letters from "two Native women" from South Africa who had spent three months in the United States headquartered at Tuskegee and who had traveled with the movable school for two weeks. Amelia Njongwana described the movable school as "practical and quite constructive . . . this is the type of work we need in our Rural Communities"[38]; while V. Sibusisiwe Makanya mentions the ten communities that they had visited and praises the personnel of the movable school for "getting down to the people they are leading and yet still hold[ing] up the ideal and the standard they are aiming at. This attitude makes them win very readily the confidence of their disciples."[39]

The movable school's "practical" and "constructive" lessons in rural uplift, then, were seen by some visitors from southern Africa as potentially adaptable to their own conditions. In his 1936 book Campbell mentions that three years after Father Harry Buck returned to Southern Rhodesia "the government of South Rhodesia started the work . . . they now have demonstrators at work in many of the native reserves," he wrote, "and many more workers in training."[40] As economic historian E. Kushinga Makombe points out, Southern Rhodesia's colonial state blamed the decline in agricultural production in the 1930s on "poor farming methods on the part of Africans instead of the skewed land distribution pattern and pernicious policies" that favored European agricultural production. As a result, the state undertook modernization measures such as the opening of new schools "where 'modern' methods of farming were taught."[41] Given this situation, it is not difficult to imagine why the state experimented with Tuskegee's movable school, assuming its practical lessons would help modernize African farmers. Southern Rhodesia's colonial state was interested in one of the goals of the movable school—"improved" agricultural production—but certainly not in another of those goals, Black land ownership. Disembedded from its roots in Tuskegee, the movable school was a useful technology for colonial administrators.

Campbell's *The Movable School Goes to the Negro Farmer* was distributed to officials in London's Colonial Office in anticipation of a 1944–1945 survey that he co-directed in Africa (see chapter 5). Margaret Wrong, one of the other two co-directors of the survey, gave a copy of the book to an official at the Colonial Office in London who had expressed interest in reading it.[42] It's not entirely clear how she knew of the book, although her longstanding interest in literacy, Africa, and her work directing the International Committee on Christian Literature for Africa suggests that the book circulated widely through those international circuits of organizations involved in rural reforms.[43] In her notes written while preparing for the survey she mentions the book several times, indicating at one point her suggestion that it should be translated into Twi, a language spoken by the Ashanti people.[44] She may have thought that Campbell's story of rural uplift could prove useful as African leaders were debating models for future rural improvement during the decolonization period. The movable school itself, as a technology of dispensing rural education, and the discourse of uplift in which that technology was situated, were also potential models for postwar colonial governance particularly in places that the Colonial Office believed were in jeopardy due to economic and social upheaval. As a range of scholars have shown, colonial officials were developing policies meant to uplift Africans through improving their standards of living and creating self-sustaining communities in order to maintain economic solvency in the United Kingdom's African colonies, though of course these circumstances and the processes of decolonization varied greatly from colony to colony.[45]

Twenty years earlier, when Beatrice Blackwood had visited Tuskegee and observed the movable school, she noted in her diary that the plantation owner, Mr. Hardy, was clear that the "prosperity of the South depended on both Negroes and Whites working together." Several days later she writes "Discussed the situation in S. Africa which seems to be as bad as it is here. The problems of the Southern States are only bits of a problem which is world-wide."[46] The "problem" that was "world-wide" was how to manage "Negroes and Whites working together" to maintain economic prosperity in the U.S. South and in South Africa. As this chapter has explained, USDA officials and colonial agents in some parts of southern Africa believed that the movable school was one such management tool. As a technology developed for and by the African American extension service of the USDA, it became a hallmark of its operations and was used by various constituencies—Washington, D.C.-based USDA officials, Tuskegee-based officials, and local agents—to legitimize and promote their activities. Depicted as almost always in motion both through space and in time (the reiterations of before and after scenes), the politics embedded in Tuskegee's movable school—how the improvements it brought to the most remote and impoverished Black farmer could eventually lead to land and home ownership—could be overlooked by white landlords and USDA state and regional officials. As a tool of uplift propaganda, and emptied of any political intent, the movable school's message of how hard work and self-help could transform problem populations reached the hallways of U.S. government buildings and the British Colonial Office. With the onset of the Great Depression, that message reverberated deeply within those hallways, and as I show in the following chapter, shaped how New Deal interventions aimed directly at Black farm ownership were operationalized within the Jim Crow South.

CHAPTER 4

# Prairie Farms and the Struggle for Black Land Ownership

When Farm Security Administration (FSA) photographer Marion Post Wolcott visited the Black resettlement community of Prairie Farms in March of 1939, she followed the mandate established by the head of the photography division—Roy Stryker—by focusing her attention on the work Prairie Farms' residents were conducting to improve their lives: children busy at school, women tending to their poultry and canning, men at the grist mill with their corn.[1] In figure 4.1, for example, Wolcott focuses on an "improved" farm family (wife and child sitting on the porch, with husband working hard to complete fencing and a gate), in front of their new whitewashed house, while figure 4.2 depicts a farm wife proudly displaying her canned goods inside her new smokehouse. The school and cooperative store that served as the sociospatial locus of Prairie Farms are also featured, displaying the ways in which the FSA was not simply about improving families but also creating improved communities (figs. 4.3, 4.4). As an African American resettlement community that was administered by a Black community manager, Coleman Camp, and that was supervised by the faculty and administration of Tuskegee Institute located less than twenty miles away, Prairie Farms was clearly a governmental experiment aimed at reforming Black lives. And as part of the propaganda effort to help legitimize that experiment, Wolcott produced photographs that depicted model Black citizens in a model Black community. And yet not long after these photographs were taken, this model community and its citizens were revealed as problematic. Coleman Camp was fired after repeated charges of mismanagement, while the community store manager, Lilla D. Brown, admitted to embezzling funds from the store and was dismissed. In fact, almost from the beginning and certainly at the time Wolcott visited Prairie Farms in 1939, FSA local, regional, and federal officials found Prairie Farms' residents and managers less than worthy, with accusations of poor management and criminality riddling the letters and memos that were sent back and forth.

**FIGURE 4.1.** Farm family posed outside of their new home. Original caption: "Front of new home of project family. He is building a gate for front yard. Prairie Farms, Alabama." Marion Post Wolcott, March 1939. Library of Congress, Prints and Photographs Division, Farm Security Administration/Office of War Information Black-and-White Negatives.

**FIGURE 4.2.** Mrs. Brown displaying her canned goods in the smokehouse. Original caption: "Mrs. Brown in her smokehouse with home-canned goods and cured meat. Prairie Farms, Alabama." Marion Post Wolcott, March 1939. Library of Congress, Prints and Photographs Division, Farm Security Administration/Office of War Information Black-and-White Negatives.

**FIGURE 4.3.** Prairie Farms Cooperative Store. Original caption: "Cooperative store. Prairie Farms, Alabama." Marion Post Wolcott, March 1939. Library of Congress, Prints and Photographs Division, Farm Security Administration/Office of War Information Black-and-White Negatives.

**FIGURE 4.4.** Prairie Farms Community Building and School. Original caption: "Community and school building. Prairie Farms, Alabama." Marion Post Wolcott, March 1939. Library of Congress, Prints and Photographs Division, Farm Security Administration/Office of War Information Black-and-White Negatives.

The disjuncture between the photographs of model citizens and the numerous accusations of less than worthy behavior suggest the contradictions that characterized the time and place of Coleman Camp and Lilla Brown: the reformist impulse on the part of New Deal officials to create model farmers and communities on the one hand, and the dystopic realities of a racialized labor system that made it impossible to thrive and in which racist assumptions of criminality were rife. Like the many other resettlement communities constructed in the early years of the New Deal, Prairie Farms was a government experiment meant to help solve the combined problems of soil degradation and rural poverty. As one of the few Black resettlement communities, that experiment bumped up against the racist realities of the Jim Crow South, with Camp and Brown bearing the brunt of that collision. Yet as this chapter will reveal, that collision and the eventual failure of the experiment at Prairie Farms bears scars that are far deeper than the failure of similar New Deal experiments elsewhere. Lost somewhere between serving as a tool for New Deal propaganda and as a sounding board for racist stereotypes is the story of Prairie Farms as the culmination of Tuskegee's long struggle to resist white supremacy through Black land ownership.[2] In other words, and as I will explain in this chapter, the story of Prairie Farms long predates the New Deal and embodied—literally and figuratively—the resistance to white supremacy that Booker T. Washington had imagined when he established Tuskegee and focused much of its work on agricultural education: and that is, the goal of self-sustaining communities of Black land-owning farmers.[3] So the fact that Prairie Farms became mired in charges of mismanagement and criminality, and that only a few of its residents were eventually able to purchase their land, must have been particularly painful to Tuskegee officials who had invested so much in its success.

This chapter brings that story into focus by analyzing the long and deep prehistory to Prairie Farms and the various ways that Tuskegee officials who were meant to oversee the construction and management of Prairie Farms navigated the almost impossible situation of creating a model community of Black land-owning farmers within the Jim Crow South where the very idea of Black land-owning farmers was self-contradictory. I document the ways in which the goals of Tuskegee and Black USDA employees to support Black land ownership—goals that were shared by Washington, D.C.-based New Deal officials—faced the realities of white supremacy and the racism that shaped assumptions about what type of people were deemed worthy of government support, and to what was lost in Prairie Farms' eventual closure. I do so by first tracing the impetus for and the long history of Black "model" communities that predate and anticipate Prairie Farms, before focusing on how and why

New Deal, USDA, and Tuskegee officials envisioned, planned, and ultimately gave up on the experiment of Prairie Farms.

## Tuskegee and the Long Historical Geography of Black Land-Owning Communities

The idea of moving "problem" populations into planned communities that are legible to the state has a long history in the United States. The "civilizing" mission carried out by the U.S. government in its establishment of the Native American reservation system, beginning in the mid-nineteenth century and carried through until today, has its roots in a U.S. settler colonialism that was imagined through the lens of the Jeffersonian "garden": self-sustaining heteropatriarchal farm families living on clearly delineated packets of land, organized around communities centered on church and school.[4] The torturous history of slavery in the United States shaped this powerful sociospatial imaginary in particular ways. In his haunting book *River of Dark Dreams: Slavery and Empire in the Cotton Kingdom*, historian Walter Johnson explained that slaveholding property—that is, enslaved peoples—was maintained on a daily basis not in written deeds or contracts but in the acts of constant communal policing, in "the way a black body on an open road provoked a question that was always already structured by a supposition."[5] A Black person out of place was assumed a criminal, a runaway, subject to immediate arrest or, worse, torture and death.

This fear that Black people were out of place was a constant undercurrent of discussions by USDA and New Deal officials concerning the problem of tenant farmers and sharecroppers. As noted in earlier chapters, a primary goal of the USDA's extension service was the modernization of agriculture, and one of the keys to that modernization process in the U.S. South was the elimination of tenant farming and sharecropping. The reformist impulses of the New Deal revived this interest in mechanizing southern agriculture and shifting land tenancy practices. Federal-level USDA officials, and others working at New Deal agencies, looked to policies that encouraged home and land ownership as solutions to the problems of southern agriculture. And yet, long before federal agencies promoted land ownership, Tuskegee's leaders had developed plans to encourage and enable poor Black farmers to purchase land.[6] As noted in chapter 1, Booker T. Washington's articulation of racial uplift contained home and land ownership as key to the primary goal of racial equity, and he and other Tuskegee leaders worked tirelessly throughout the late nineteenth and early twentieth centuries to actualize that objective. For example, in the first decade of the twentieth century, Washington supervised the construction of a residential community that came to be called Greenwood Village on two hundred acres north of Tuskegee's campus.[7] It was meant to be a model Negro village that would show local farmers and visitors alike the possibilities of uplift: African Americans living in single-family homes, in a community with paved and lighted roads, complete with a city park and school for children. Washington established the Greenwood Village Improvement Society to ensure that the norms of respectable middle-class life were maintained in the village (no alcohol was permitted, yards were meant to be tidy, and so forth), with residents monitoring one another and reporting infractions. Harlan's summary of the purpose that the village was meant to serve is apt: "If Tuskegee was a preparation for life, and for assimilation into the mainstream of American life, as Washington strongly believed, then Greenwood was that life in miniature."[8] And although the homes were offered for sale to African Americans living in the area, most of the village was occupied by Tuskegee faculty who in essence became full-time proponents of uplift; during the day, as teachers in formal classrooms, and, at night, as live demonstrators of American middle-class culture.

The early twentieth century witnessed additional plans devised by Washington and others at Tuskegee to enable Black tenants to buy suitable land in the areas surrounding Tuskegee in Macon County.[9] Most of these plans were formulated as communities, that is the lands were adjoining and they were supervised by a manager who was trained at Tuskegee. Like Greenwood Village, Washington considered these model communities that would serve as object lessons to surrounding farmers. For example, as early as 1901 a joint Hampton-Tuskegee initiative called the Southern Improvement Company purchased four thousand acres of land in Macon County and offered it for sale to Black tenant farmers.[10] The community was operated on a cooperative basis, and in addition to farm homes, it included a grist mill, cotton gin, saw mill, and a school, and a Tuskegee graduate was appointed the company manager.[11] Although the experiment proved financially unviable, and the land was sold in 1919, the idea of establishing a community of land-owning African American farmers in Macon County as a form of uplift lived on at Tuskegee. Booker T. Washington retried the experiment in 1914, establishing the Tuskegee Farm and Improvement Company. The company purchased what was considered better lands in western Macon County and added an important criterion: each farmer had to be a graduate of Tuskegee. What became known as Baldwin Farms (named in honor of a Tuskegee trustee, William H. Baldwin Jr., who had helped finance the project) operated in a similar manner to the earlier development; it was under cooperative management and was supervised by a company manager who was also a graduate of Tuskegee. To what degree it can be considered a success or not is debatable, but as Zabawa and Warren point out, the last lands belonging to the company weren't sold until 1949.[12]

With the initiation of Roosevelt's New Deal programs and the promise of federal support for rural reform, Tuskegee's leaders saw new opportunities for assisting Black farmers to buy productive farmland in Macon County. In early 1934, Thomas Campbell and other Tuskegee leaders held a conference on the possibility of establishing subsistence homesteads—the name of the New Deal initiative meant to provide loans and other forms of assistance to rural regions—and put forward Baldwin Farms as a potential Subsistence Homestead project given that it was, as they wrote, "more or less already organized, and also since it is a purely Negro project ... no racial condition has to be overcome."[13] Well aware of the potential funding and support that would come from federal sponsorship, Tuskegee leaders proposed to simplify matters for officials of the Subsistence Homestead Division of the Department of the Interior by offering them an already-established community of Black farmers organized into cooperatives. In addition, Washington, D.C. officials would not need to contend with Jim Crow laws given that the community was already racially segregated. The conveners of the conference suggested that the further development of Baldwin Farms could serve "as an experiment, the idea would be to develop a high type of community life," and that "this nucleus can best serve as an incentive and stimulus for the projecting of a more desirable agricultural interest and development in other sections."[14] In other words, this community would provide a model for the rest of the region; similar in purpose to the accomplishments of the movable school. Tuskegee leaders believed that the support of the federal government would secure Baldwin Farms and further their aims of uplift and development in the region, and they gathered testimonies from those familiar with the project—including a letter from Laura R. Daly—to reinforce their claims.[15]

This proposal—to turn Baldwin Farms into a Subsistence Homestead project—was not taken up by Washington, D.C. officials, although some officials were keen on moving forward with it. They described it as a "Negro rural rehabilitation experiment" that was "regarded by both white and colored leaders as the 'way out' for the Negro whose economic status is serious and growing worse through being crowded out of industry by whites and out of agriculture by cotton reduction program."[16] Nonetheless, when federal support for a resettlement plan in Macon County was finally realized, the selected site was not Baldwin Farms but an area of more than three thousand acres just south of it, what came to be called Prairie Farms.[17]

A 1935 Resettlement Administration (RA) memo summarizing these earlier plans draws out two of the ideas that the experiments of the Southern Improvement Society and Baldwin Farms had already tested. First, it discusses the introduction of cooperatives as necessary for developing the project and suggests these cooperatives will need Tuskegee supervision: "In view of the fact that this is a Colored project, devoted exclusively to agriculture, it will be necessary to organize the following cooperative associations, which, it is planned, will be in close conjunction and cooperation with the Tuskegee Institute."[18] In other words, Black farmers were not deemed capable of conducting proper farming on their own; instead they would be organized into cooperatives and would need assistance and oversight from Tuskegee. Local Resettlement Administration's official Taylor Miller wrote in a memo outlining the terms of the government loan to establish the cooperative, "Since the project is to be occupied wholly by Negroes, the Tuskegee Institute, located only 16 miles away, is greatly interested in it and has promised to assist with the supervision of the client-families."[19] Second, as the memo indicates, the Resettlement Administration was not only investing in farmers, they were also investing in communities: "It is planned to construct educational, recreational and communal facilities."[20] Thus, the Resettlement Administration was reinforcing ideas already put forth by Tuskegee; that is, that uplifting Black farmers could be operationalized through supervised resettlement communities organized through a cooperative structure.

Planning for what eventually became Prairie Farms occurred at Tuskegee in late 1934. Drawing on ideas put forth by New Deal agencies, Campbell, President Moton, and other Tuskegee officials proposed to representatives of the Agricultural Adjustment Administration—a New Deal program whose primary goal was to assist farmers by raising agricultural commodity prices—that a large swathe of unproductive farmland known locally as the Big Hungry should be purchased by the government and put into other uses, while the tenant farmers residing there would be resettled.[21] The Tuskegee Land Utilization Project was formalized in December of 1934; the federal government bought approximately ten thousand acres of farmland that Campbell and others had deemed "submarginal," a term borrowed from the discipline of economics by New Deal officials to describe a range of agricultural conditions that would not allow for profitability.[22] Those ten thousand acres eventually became the Tuskegee National Forest. Additionally, with support from the Resettlement Administration the government purchased 3,200 acres of more productive farmland—the site of two former cotton plantations—in western Macon County and resettled many of the 133 families who had been displaced from the tract of submarginal land in the newly named community of Prairie

Farms, with the other families leaving the area on their own or with some assistance provided through government rehabilitation loans.[23]

## Imagining Prairie Farms

Hence, the resettlement community of Prairie Farms was at least as much the result of the work of Tuskegee leaders as it was New Deal officials. It represented the culmination of a long series of attempts by Tuskegee leaders to create a community of Black land-owning farmers in Macon County, and it was Tuskegee officials who put forward the idea to New Deal officials and who agreed to oversee its development. Its success, therefore, was measured not only by federal officials according to New Deal account books, but also by Tuskegee leaders according to the ideology and aesthetics of uplift. In its early planning, Resettlement Administration officials understood this joint purpose. Regional director Robert W. Hudgens wrote to Rexford Tugwell, the director of the Resettlement Administration, in May of 1936 outlining the importance of Prairie Farms as an agent of improvement not only for the designated families, but also for the region and the race: "We feel that this project will not only tremendously help the sixty resettlement families, but will offer facilities of all kinds to all negro families in the section and will be of an educational value to the Tuskegee Institute and the negro race."[24] Like the farms rebuilt with the help of the movable school, Prairie Farms was to serve as an object lesson of uplift for the entire community. The original architectural plans for the design of the community called for two- and three-bedroom houses complete with indoor plumbing and enclosed work porches, set in acreage divided into various uses—the land close to the residences would be divided into gardens, orchards, barnyard, poultry houses and laundry court, while the fields would consist of cotton, hay, corn, and pasture (figs. 4.5, 4.6). Thus, the plan was for comfortable, modern dwellings surrounded by fields that would provide for self-sufficiency as well as cash cropping through cotton production—a perfect material outcome of uplift ideology.

The preliminary documents regarding the formation of the cooperative association that was to govern the economic activities at Prairie Farms are similar in tone, promoting the association as beneficial to the entire community. Katharine Deitz, the Resettlement Administration's regional educational advisor, assessed Prairie Farms as the "most outstanding negro project in the Region to justify a cooperative," because "Tuskegee Institute has agreed to use the school and community center as a demonstration, not only in teacher-

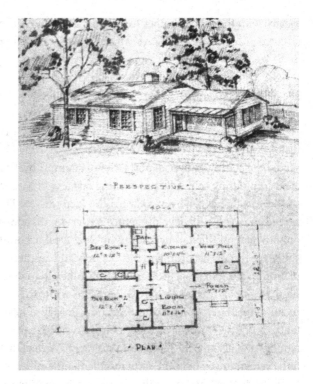

**FIGURE 4.5.** Perspective and plan for Prairie Farms two-bedroom farmhouse with enclosed work porch and bathroom. RG 96, box 74, National Archives, College Park, Md.

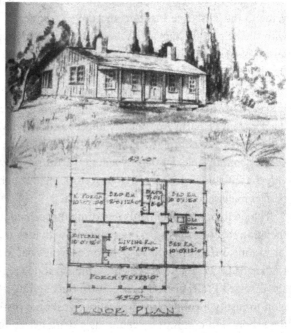

**FIGURE 4.6.** Perspective and plan for Prairie Farms three-bedroom farmhouse with two chimneys, enclosed porch, and bathroom. RG 96, box 74, National Archives, College Park, Md.

training, but as a way of living for rural communities. With this group of students from the Institute in close touch with the cooperative of the project, it may mean the stimulation and promotion, not only of communities like this, throughout the State and South, but also of cooperatives."[25] Thus Prairie Farms would serve as a material model not only of Black uplift but also of the value of rural communities operating through cooperatives. As Tuskegee's presidents Washington and Moton had earlier surmised, establishing cooperatives was key to Black farming success: it allowed farmers to purchase supplies at lower costs and gave them competitive advantages in the marketing of their products. When the loan to operationalize the cooperative association came through in 1938, now officially from the Farm Security Administration instead of the Resettlement Administration, the documents specified that in addition to forming cooperative associations for purchases and marketing, the cooperative would make possible the construction of a grist mill and the purchase of large farm equipment. This would, importantly, lower farmers' production costs. The documents suggested that the loans were figured such that repayment was eminently affordable on the part of the farm families, with expectations that every family would earn a surplus each year. Each family's loan payment for their home was also figured generously. In other words, the government saw no reason why the families chosen to live at Prairie Farms would not succeed economically, with the expectation that after five years they would be able to purchase their own home and land from the government.[26]

To ensure that the community was indeed a success, the families were chosen carefully, with the USDA's Tuskegee-based officials doing the vetting. Writing in general about the extension service's work during this time, Campbell summarized the situation thus: "It became the duty of the Negro Extension agents to assist the white agents in alleviating want among scores of relief clients through resettlement and rehabilitation agencies. Since only a limited number of farmers can be accommodated by the RA the extension service has been extremely careful to certify only the most deserving and those who have demonstrated the greatest promise of succeeding."[27] In other words, like most resettlement communities, the "settlers" of Prairie Farms were carefully vetted so as to ensure that the government's loans would be paid back and that the "character" of the affected families would represent the American ideal: a heteropatriarchal nuclear family.

A series of photographs taken by P. H. Polk, Tuskegee's official photographer and head of its Photography Department, provided documentation of the range of rural living and farming conditions that characterized the land that was to be resettled.[28] The selection and labeling of the images makes clear the ways in which families were judged in terms of potential resettlement clients. A photograph of what is labeled "rundown fields" depicts in the distance a corn-producing field with the caption querying whether this is "the last spot in an 'eighty' where crops can grow," suggesting that the area is now deemed submarginal, that is, no longer capable of supporting any substantial farming activities (fig. 4.7). The label "submarginal" was also applied to the people who worked that land, as is evident in the original caption for figure 4.8, a photograph that focuses on a small, evidently run-down, one-room cabin (note the missing roofing material and the uneven logs and clapboard siding). The woman barely discernible at the far left of the image is presumably so poor that she doesn't own a wash line and is forced to hang her laundry over a shabby fence. A more affluent family is documented in figure 4.9; the clapboard-sided house is in good repair and a wash line stretches out to the right of the image. But as the original caption suggests, this is a family of declining fortunes, and it's not clear if this family will be resettled or not: "'Perplexed'—Home Too Good To Leave, No Husband—No Workstock—Six Minor Children." A photograph poignantly titled "leaving" (fig. 4.10) focuses on a family posed outside their modest slightly ramshackle house with their possessions loaded onto the horses and wagon next to them. Depicted in the background is a significantly larger and more ornate home, presumably that of the plantation owner, clear evidence that this family are tenant farmers who are "leaving" poor farming conditions. Taken together these photographs provided the "before" to the imagined bright "after" that Prairie Farms promised—new, modern homes, fertile land, a community with productive, educational, and recreational activities—thus operationalizing uplift ideology.

### Living Prairie Farms

Since the archival documents do not specify the names of the families who were resettled from the Big Hungry, nor do the photographs provide family names, it is not possible to say with certainty which, if any, of these families were moved to Prairie Farms. But for the thirty plus families who were chosen, their living conditions certainly improved. Marion Post Wolcott's 1939 FSA photographs of Prairie Farms portray hard-working Black farm families living in new, whitewashed homes (figs. 4.1, 4.2). Wolcott took this series of photographs on one of her early visits to the South, assigned by Roy Stryker to produce photographs of FSA projects that highlighted its many successes. For much of this trip she traveled with Constance Daniel, a senior administra-

**FIGURE 4.7.** Photograph of remnants of farming area near Tuskegee. Original caption: "Exhibit VIII. Rundown Fields. The Last Spot in an 'Eighty' where crops can grow? (10 bu. corn per acre)." P. H. Polk, Campbell Collection, Tuskegee University Archives, Tuskegee University.

**FIGURE 4.8.** Photograph of a small home with a woman and child hanging laundry outside. Original caption: "Exhibit XI Submarginal People—'Home Sweet Home.'" P. H. Polk, Campbell Collection, Tuskegee University Archives, Tuskegee University.

**FIGURE 4.9.** A woman with children posed outside a farmhouse. Original caption: "Exhibit XIV 'Perplexed'—Home Too Good To Leave, No Husband—No Workstock—Six Minor Children." P. H. Polk, Campbell Collection, Tuskegee University Archives, Tuskegee University.

**FIGURE 4.10.** Family posed outside of their small farm home with a horse and wagon loaded with household possessions. Original caption: "Leaving." P. H. Polk, Campbell Collection, Tuskegee University Archives, Tuskegee University.

tive assistant with the FSA assigned to advise and evaluate its Black rehabilitation programs.[29] Daniel, a highly educated Black woman with an undergraduate degree from Atlanta University and a teaching certificate from Tuskegee, had asked Stryker for a photographer to accompany her while she evaluated Gee's Bend, another FSA Black project not far from Prairie Farms.[30] Although it is not clear if Daniel visited Prairie Farms with Wolcott, documents suggest that Wolcott consulted with Daniel about her visit there.[31] Before her employment with the FSA, Constance Daniel and her husband Victor (also a graduate of Tuskegee) had been the founding principles at a Catholic institute in southern Maryland, an institution modeled on Tuskegee's educational philosophy of self-help. Well aware of the publicity purpose of her trip—to provide evidence of the "before and after" success stories of the FSA—and steeped in the uplift ideology of Tuskegee, Daniel would have wanted images that documented Black self-sufficiency and community-building.[32] And certainly Wolcott's photographs do just that. The photographs make clear that these families' lives have been greatly improved. No longer tenants living in shacks on plantations, these families now resided in a community that is centered on a school and cooperative store (figs. 4.3, 4.4). Most adults are pictured in action; feeding their livestock, working on improvements to their home, delivering grain to the newly built grist mill, while children are shown engaged in recreational and educational activities (figs. 4.11, 4.12). The photograph of a Mrs. Brown in a smokehouse surrounded by the canned goods that she has presumably worked hard to produce (fig. 4.2) fulfilled Stryker's mandate to document the FSA's goals and speaks to the USDA's long history of using such images to promote and legitimize the Home Demonstration Unit of its extension service (see chapter 2). Here, Mrs. Brown represents the goal of Black extension work: a proper farm wife, creating a healthy and self-sufficient labor force through hard work.

Yet Wolcott's photographs also make clear that the reality of living at Prairie Farms was different from its imagined plans. The homes, for example, are scaled back considerably from the 1936 plans. All of them are simple four-room houses built from basic wooden materials, and importantly, unlike the proposed plans for Prairie Farms and unlike the actual homes of white RA communities, none of the houses had indoor plumbing facilities.[33] The degree to which living in Prairie Farms contrasted with its original articulation becomes even clearer in the records of its Cooperative Association. The Prairie Farms Cooperative Association was incorporated simultaneously with the resettlement plan, yet almost from its inception the association was in trouble with the government. The official authorization for the government loan

FIGURE 4.11. A man with children posed on a wagon with oxen in front of the Prairie Farms Grist Mill. Original caption: "Cooperative grist mill. Prairie Farms, Alabama." Marion Post Wolcott, March 1939. Library of Congress, Prints and Photographs Division, Farm Security Administration/Office of War Information Black-and-White Negatives.

FIGURE 4.12. A classroom in the Prairie Farms school. Original caption: "Classroom showing varying ages of students in primary grades in school. Prairie Farms, Alabama." Marion Post Wolcott, March 1939. Library of Congress, Prints and Photographs Division, Farm Security Administration/Office of War Information Black-and-White Negatives.

that would fund cooperative activities did not make its way through the bureaucracy until mid-July 1938, and less than a year later some warning bells were already being rung.[34] In April of 1939, the same month that Marion Post Wolcott visited Prairie Farms, the director of the Resettlement Division of the Farm Security Administration, J. O. Walker, wrote to his regional director based in Montgomery—E. S. Morgan—that "there has been no satisfactory relation between the gross profit on sales and the expenses of the Association" and accordingly he asked for an investigation of the matter "with great thoroughness" so that he could know "what this organization proposed to do to correct these conditions."[35] Given that the government had provided the money through a loan to support the cooperative, officials expected astute management and eventual loan repayments. Over the next several years similar letters were exchanged between FSA administrators and between those administrators and the community managers at Prairie Farms, Coleman Camp and Gladstone Hodge, outlining financial and management problems with the association. Evident in this series of letters is the growing concern on the part of New Deal officials that the cooperative was not being managed correctly.

Apparently, Morgan shared the April 1939 letter from Walker with the Prairie Farms' manager and board of directors. He reported to Will Alexander, head of the FSA, in June of that year that "Major Walker's letter was timely, and just what was needed to get action at Prairie Farms. The tendency of Negro personnel at Prairie Farms has been to adopt 'rule of thumb' methods and follow them without any consideration of improvements. Also, personnel have been lax in trying to sell a cooperative movement, and have tended towards giving in to members and to outside trade on policies of credit, prices, services, etc."[36] Exactly what those "rule of thumb" methods are was not outlined, but presumably they were not the modern methods FSA administrators preferred. More details about those methods can be discerned in a letter that Coleman Camp, the manager of Prairie Farms, wrote to Taylor Miller outlining exactly how the cooperative association was responding to Miller's earlier requests. In this detailed letter dated September 5, 1939, Camp lists activities by category: hay baling, cattle enterprise, farm shop, store, feed and grist mill, and heavy equipment. A sampling of these activities is telling. Under the category of *Cattle Enterprise*, for example, Camp writes, "cattle to be observed three times a week, cattle to be salted once a week, pasture fence to be checked once a week, all cooperative cattle to be branded as soon as possible"; while under the category of *Store* he writes, "to meet competition and not adopt the practice of underselling, to keep accurate records, to extend no credit to nonmembers, to reduce all expenses to a minimum."[37] Camp, in other words, is trying to assure administrators that the rule of thumb methods will be replaced by modern ones. Apparently, these new methods were followed for a period of time. In December of 1940, Miller writes a congratulatory letter to Camp, stating that "a true association exists only when members, directors, and officers take responsibility, and it is good to learn that by taking responsibility the Association has sufficient feed to carry all the cattle it has through the winter, and to buy more and also carry them."[38]

But Miller's satisfaction with Camp's management style was partial and short-lived. The community store became a focus for Miller and other FSA local and regional supervisors who were concerned that it seemed to be losing money, or at least not profiting as it should be. A series of letters between regional supervisor E. S. Morgan and FSA Washington, D.C.-based officials in the spring and summer of 1940 repeatedly mention the low profit margin for the store, and suggest that the store was either being mismanaged or was subject to theft.[39] To deter shoplifting, Morgan suggested that the internal arrangement of the store should be rearranged so that customers could not directly access goods, similar to what the store manager had accomplished at the other Black resettlement community in Alabama, Gee's Bend.[40] Yet matters did not seem to improve, and reached a nadir the following year when the store began to post monthly losses. In February of 1941, Miller admonished Camp for lack of accountability in regard to merchandise that had gone missing at the store, ending his letter with, "Do you and the Board of Directors intend to permit this problem to continue?"[41] Miller's concerns over store losses increased the next month when yet more merchandise went missing, and he concluded that store manager Brown needed better training and organizational skills in order to continue as manager. "Miss Brown has never had complete charge of farm supplies so that directors could place responsibility on her," Miller wrote, adding "she does not know how to price invoices, and admits errors in inventory, in pricing and in other simple operating problems."[42] As it turns out, Miller's assumptions regarding Brown's incompetence were misplaced. In August 1941, when Lilla Brown admitted to embezzling $198 from the store and taking $69.42 worth of merchandise for her own personal use, she indicated that she did so on purpose and in defiance of not being granted the salary increase that she had asked for. According to the investigator's report, "When the Board of Directors refused to increase her salary until the store was placed on a profit-making basis, Lilla D. Brown verbally admitted that she became careless, carefree, and defiant of directors' orders."[43] She was promptly dismissed from her job.

Other apparent mismanagement issues were highlighted by FSA supervisors who expressed their dismay at what they called "the apparent complete inability to grasp the simplest fundamental of good business practice necessary to their management of their own business."[44] Less than a year later, Taylor Miller wrote a scathing letter to Camp: "Plans for controlling operations of cooperative associations were outlined at our Ft. Valley conference. Such plans would put you in position to exercise administrative supervision over operations of the Prairie Farms Association so that income would always cover expenses and leave a balance as profit. The October accounting report of the Prairie Farms Association indicates about as poor a job of administrative supervision as could be possible." His list of examples of that poor job is long and begins with, "the store enterprise paid $862.49 for merchandise then sold it for $738.48, or $132 less than it paid for the goods . . . at the same time, loss of merchandise that cannot be accounted for increased by nearly $400."[45] Several months later Camp received a letter from Miller's supervisor chastising him for not responding to Miller's concerns: "We plan for results and we expect results. If you cannot carry out plans as outlined, we expect you to so advise us rather than to jeopardize the program with silences."[46] Still without any satisfactory response, Miller writes again to Camp in March of 1942 outlining the failures of the cooperative association, "Prairie Farms Cooperative Association has not established operations on a sound financial basis . . . the feed and grist mill and heavy equipment enterprises have not been liquidated." Threatening to appoint a government supervisor, Miller writes: "This informs you that unless the feed and grist mill and heavy equipment enterprises are liquidated within one month, and unless sound business policies are adopted and approved by this office to guide the management of the Association's affairs, it will be my recommendation that the Government exercise its right to appoint a supervisor as its representative to carry out terms of the loan agreement."[47]

Within two weeks Miller was already discussing with his supervisors the idea of replacing Camp with Henry Quinn, another member of the association, saying that, "if he receives proper training, and follows good business practices until thoroughly familiar with them, he should supply the management needs that have always been lacking at Prairie Farms."[48] Apparently that suggestion was not met with approval, because by late 1942 Gladstone Hodge—a man who previously had been hired as a spy in the cooperative store to determine who or what was behind the losses of merchandise—was being addressed in memos as the cooperative manager.[49] With Hodge at the helm, Miller believed it was now time to embark on what he called "an educational program" for all those directly involved with Prairie Farms—its "board of directors, members and employees." "We must teach these people to do things for themselves," Miller writes, "however, we want to follow your suggestions as to how it should be handled."[50] The first step in this program was a mapping exercise. Miller planned on providing a layout map of Prairie Farms and asking the board of directors to "take a list of the membership and indicate on the map the location of each member's unit."[51] For those members not residing on the project, a county map would be provided and again the board was to indicate the location of members' homes. Why this exercise was considered important is not entirely clear, though less than a year later it became apparent that the FSA was missing important geospatial information.

Miller's new geographical education program hardly had time to effect any sort of sought-after change in management style; by April of 1943, with the New Deal government under attack for what some believed was its socialist leanings, cooperatives were a first casualty, and FSA administrators were already planning the liquidation of most cooperatives including Prairie Farms Cooperative Association.[52] In the memo accompanying the financial documents concerning the association, Miller writes to his supervisors that as of January 1945 the liquidation that was called for in 1943 has yet to be completed because "we have never been able to locate all the members, and it has been difficult to obtain signatures of some members that could be located."[53] Even in these last documents, therefore, the problematic nature of Prairie Farms' members and occupants was highlighted: some could not write or refused to comply; many were not spatially legible.

Prairie Farms was in many senses typical of New Deal resettlement communities and cooperatives. The degree to which these communities succeeded measured in terms of economic stability, social cohesion, or land conservation is still a highly contested issue. Most southern rural communities like Prairie Farms enabled a small number of sharecroppers and tenant farmers to own their own land, but never succeeded in creating structural changes to the racist agricultural labor system.[54] As this series of correspondence makes clear, however, the fact that this was one of only nine Black communities marks it in particular ways. First, as I pointed out earlier, part of the rationale for establishing Prairie Farms and thereby betting on its success was the fact that it would be managed by officials of Tuskegee Institute. In early planning documents, when the discussions were regarding establishing a subsistence homestead project, what became Prairie Farms was singled out: "In view of the fact that this is a Colored project, devoted exclusively to agriculture, it will be necessary to organize the following cooperative associations, which, it is planned, will be in close conjunction and cooperation with the Tuskegee Institute."⁵⁵ In other words, New Deal officials believed that unlike similar white resettlement communities, Prairie Farms required oversight to ensure that its farmers would conduct themselves in an appropriate manner. Second, when New Deal officials were not satisfied with the activities and management of the cooperative association, their dissatisfaction was shaped by racist notions of cultural norms. E. S. Morgan's 1939 letter to Will Alexander points to the "Negro personnel" who adopt "rule of thumb" methods of management and who are "giving in" to "outside" ways of doing business, that is, to Black ways of doing business;⁵⁶ while Miller expresses his frustration over mismanagement with his last-ditch effort to teach "these people" how to help themselves.⁵⁷

And yet perhaps most important, as a project of improvement and modernization, Prairie Farms was intended to do much more than provide better land for Black farmers. Like home demonstration work and the movable school, Campbell and others at Tuskegee, and federal-level RA and FSA officials, hoped Prairie Farms would succeed in helping Black farmers move out of tenancy and would serve as an experiment in Black collective community-making. It was intended not only as a model of modern farming practices, but also of an idealized American community joined through collective economic activity and common goals that aligned with racial uplift. Like most other rural New Deal resettlement communities, the FSA constructed a school in addition to the farm homes. At Prairie Farms the school also functioned as a community and healthcare center, and New Deal officials made clear that this center was to serve more than just the families living on the project given that there were few educational or medical facilities for African Americans in the area. The New Deal investment in Prairie Farms therefore included funds for the construction of a school that would serve students not only in Prairie Farms but also in the surrounding community, and funds to help support a fulltime nurse and visiting doctor who were also meant to provide health care to the entire community. As noted earlier, regional director R. W. Hudgens wrote to Tugwell in 1936, saying that the project "will offer facilities of all kinds to all negro families in the section and will be of an educational value to the Tuskegee Institute and the negro race."⁵⁸ After a visit to Prairie Farms in March of 1939, the FSA chief medical officer and regional education advisor discovered that there were no provisions in place to provide health care for the other Black families in need in the rest of Macon County; as a result they determined that when the FSA appointed a nurse to Prairie Farms she would also serve the surrounding community: "It is understood that the appointment of a Negro nurse for Prairie Farms has been authorized, although the final selection of a nurse has not yet been made. It is felt that such a nurse should extend her activities beyond the small number of Project families."[59]

The educational facilities too served the broader community; in its first year, there were 213 students enrolled in the school, more than the number of children living on the project and considerably more than was intended, given that the school had a 175-seat capacity. That Coleman Camp devoted most of his 1939 summary of project activities to what he called, "Our Educational Viewpoint," indicates the importance of the school and its broader activities to him and what he considered his job as community manager.[60] Those broader activities of the school are made clear both in the design of the building (in addition to classrooms, it included a farm shop, facilities to teach home economics, and a health clinic) and in Camp's opening remarks defining the community's educational viewpoint: "You may note that we have said community as well as educational program. This is true since we believe that if education is to be of any use, it must be based on all the experiences of life, so certainly, living together as a community is of primary importance. We cannot separate in our thinking the work of the parents of the community from that of the children, because education does not stop after one leaves school." Camp, a graduate of Tuskegee, was echoing the mantra of Tuskegee's educational program; that is, the goal of education is to provide training for particular occupations, but also to inculcate social and cultural norms. Camp's comments highlight how the entirety of Prairie Farms—its cooperatives, living arrangements, housing facilities—not just its school, was meant as an educational program, training Black farm families how to adhere to Progressive-era models of modern citizens. Far from the communist cooperatives that many critics dubbed these experiments of the Resettlement Administration, communities like Prairie Farms represented idealized American norms of family and community life: private home and land ownership, heteropatriarchal families, shared community values. At the top of his list for what he hoped the educational program would accomplish in the following year, Camp wrote: "To develop better citizenship through the realization of the necessity that each must play his part in making a happy community."[61]

Thus, unlike white FSA resettlement communities, the liquidation of Prairie Farms had impacts far beyond the families who lived there. Without funding from the federal government, Tuskegee did its best to maintain the educational facilities at the school with all the services it provided—health clinic, community center, recreational center. It was able to retain the educational facilities, assisted by state funding, all the way through to 1972, while the building's other uses were foreclosed.[62] For Tuskegee officials like Campbell, Prairie

Farms continued to be used as material evidence of uplift. For example, one of the many overseas visitors whom he hosted at Tuskegee after his return from Africa was a British Anglican missionary, C. Murray Rogers, whom he had met in London before returning to the United States.[63] He provided Rogers with a tour of the rural area around Tuskegee, including what Campbell called "the improved FSA houses in which these colored farmers are living, as compared with the run-down shacks out of which they had recently moved." Rogers was "particularly impressed."[64] During the same tour Campbell took Rogers to Dallas County to visit the farm of Fred Smith who, in Campbell's words, had "really caught the spirit of the Extension Service" and who embodies "leadership ability, cooperation, thrift and determination." The accompanying photographs of Smith's old home and new home make clear that the "before and after" trope that characterizes the aesthetics of uplift were in full operation (figs. 4.13, 4.14). But they also serve as important reminders of the politics of racial uplift; Black land-owning farmers like Smith were direct threats to the white land-owning elites of Dallas County. Like at least some of the farmers at Prairie Farms, Fred Smith had moved from a tenant farmer to a landowner with the visible evidence of uplift in full view: a new farm home.

## After Prairie Farms

For Washington, D.C.–based officials, the experiment of Prairie Farms, then, was one of a long list of similar experiments meant to solve the problem of tenant farming in the South. For Tuskegee leaders, it was a material manifestation of uplift ideology. As I've shown here, from the time of Booker T. Washington onward, Tuskegee officials had imagined and at times put into place communities of land-owning farmers who were governed by strict rules of conduct. These communities were seen as exemplars of uplift, as both the outcome of hard work and self-help, and the impetus for further uplift among others. What distinguishes Prairie Farms from these other similar experiments in rural living is the direct involvement of New Deal agencies and the fact that Tuskegee's leaders became enmeshed in those agencies' networks of local, state, and regional officials. As such, the story of Prairie Farms shows how Tuskegee officials used the New Deal to actively support Black tenant farmers and to further their goals of Black farm ownership, thus shifting traditional New Deal scholarship that positions federal-level officials as the main actors of improvement projects. Campbell and others at Tuskegee intervened in federal-level, New Deal, decision making in order to further their

**FIGURE 4.13.** Fred Smith's old home. Original caption: "Dallas County, Alabama—November 1, 1945. Reading l. to r. Rev. G. Murray Rogers, S. W. Boynton, County Agent, N. Kollock, District Agent and Miss L. N. Upshaw, Home Demonstration Agent, standing in front of the original home of Farmer Fred Smith, which is being demolished and salvaged for use in constructing the new home. Picture below shows the new home nearing completion." Thomas Campbell, "Report of Field Trips and Other Activities, 1945," Campbell Collection, Tuskegee University Archives, Tuskegee University.

**FIGURE 4.14.** Fred Smith's new home under construction. Thomas Campbell, "Report of Field Trips and Other Activities, 1945," Campbell Collection, Tuskegee University Archives, Tuskegee University.

goal of helping Black tenant farmers become landowners and to support self-sustaining communities of uplifted Black farmers, a goal that, as this chapter has documented, long preceded the establishment of the Resettlement Administration and the New Deal. It was Campbell and Tuskegee President Moton who originally approached Agricultural Adjustment Act officials regarding the possibility of establishing a resettlement community of Black farmers in Macon County, having already formulated a process through which land could be purchased and families resettled. Thus, they were able to use one of the least helpful New Deal agencies in regard to assisting Black tenants and sharecroppers—the Agricultural Adjustment Administration—as an entry point into negotiations with regional and federal officials that eventually led to the establishment of Prairie Farms, fulfilling their long-term goal of securing better land for Black farmers.[65]

As a rural resettlement community composed of and managed entirely by Black citizens—its manager and board of trustees were Black—and overseen by Tuskegee, Prairie Farms also documents the pervasive and insidious ways that race and racism shaped federal-level programs like the RA and FSA. Katznelson's commanding analysis of how the New Deal was shaped by Roosevelt's capitulations to southern Democrats and therefore to the policies of Jim Crow contextualizes that racism within the realm of international, national, and regional politics.[66] The story of Prairie Farms documents its lived effects. Unlike white resettlement communities, New Deal officials assumed that Prairie Farms required the oversight of Tuskegee officials, thus validating local white elites' racist beliefs. And unlike white resettlement communities, the facilities established at Prairie Farms were meant to impact the wider Black community, to uplift the race and the selected farm families. Thus, when Prairie Farms was liquidated and the community and healthcare services were closed, the entire Black population of the surrounding county felt the negative impacts. And when the experiment was in danger of failing from mismanagement the blame was placed squarely on the manager and his board of directors who as "Negro personnel" had adopted "rule of thumb" methods of operation.[67] The solution to these failures was sought in yet further intervention, in teaching "these people how to help themselves" through a new educational program that was to begin with a mapping exercise.[68] That plan was forestalled by the liquidation of Prairie Farms, but the impetus behind it lived (and lives) on in the many other rural improvement projects that scholars have documented.

Development, as Tania Li argues, is always deferred; the distance between the imagined, future, "modern" citizens and communities and the realities of racial and economic hierarchies never bridged. Like many other subjects of state intervention projects before and after her, Lilla D. Brown's life was powerfully shaped by the state's "will to improve."[69] Her position as the store manager must have afforded her the respect of the community, and no doubt must have resulted from community leaders' high assessments of her management skills and respectability. And yet, placed under the surveillance of FSA officials and subject to the racial disciplining of the state, Brown was deemed unworthy of state sponsorship, initially because she was assumed to be incompetent and then later—through her act of defiance—labeled a criminal. Her fall from grace, like Camp's, was precipitous and disastrous, fired from her job and source of financial support.

Both Lilla Brown's and Coleman Camp's lives were trapped in the unbridgeable distance between the imagined Prairie Farms and the real Prairie Farms, between the project of improvement and its ever-deferral. Chosen as leaders in their community and object lessons of the power of uplift, their lives and accomplishments were nonetheless sullied with charges of criminality and wrongdoing. Tuskegee's leaders' long-held goal of creating communities of Black land-owning farmers collided with the realities of living in the Jim Crow South and the racism that inflected federal-level projects of improvement as those projects were put into operation locally. The story of Prairie Farms—from its inception as a Tuskegee-conceived plan for community-building to its failure at generating economic and social results in the eyes of FSA officials—is an object lesson of how local collective action confronts state projects of improvement, sometimes successfully and sometimes not. At Prairie Farms, Tuskegee's discourse of uplift encountered the New Deal's discourse of development.[70] The next chapter provides further documentation of that encounter.

## CHAPTER 5

# Black Extension Work in the U.S. South and Liberal Development Overseas

In September of 1944, Thomas Campbell arrived in Africa with Jackson Davis, associate director of the General Education Board, a philanthropic organization funded by the Rockefeller family, and Margaret Wrong who worked with the International Missionary Council, in order to conduct a survey of educational facilities, missions, and rural development. In the preface to their book *Africa Advancing* that they wrote soon after returning home, Davis, Campbell, and Wrong stated the goal of their trip modestly: to undertake "a study of education and agriculture in West Africa and the Belgian Congo."[1] On the face of it, Campbell was certainly an unusual choice to co-direct this survey. He had no prior experience or expertise in regard to African education, missions, resources, or agriculture—the intended goals of the trip—nor was he a prominent Black educator. And although his work was based at Tuskegee Institute, he did not work for Tuskegee but instead for the USDA. If Davis and others at the Rockefeller Foundation were interested in promulgating the industrial form of education that Tuskegee was known for, they most certainly would have chosen one of Tuskegee's many professors. Their choice of Campbell suggests that they were looking for something else; not experience and expertise in industrial education per se, but in another form of "education," one that was being dispensed by the USDA's African American agricultural extension service, whose practices I have documented in the preceding four chapters.

As Campbell and his co-directors were preparing for their trip to Africa, the head of the USDA's cooperative extension service—M. L. Wilson—was busy hosting a conference in Washington, D.C. that made clear the importance of the practices of his agency in the postwar era. Wilson stated in his opening address that the primary goal of the conference—titled "The Contribution of Extension Methods and Techniques Toward the Rehabilitation of War-Torn Countries"—was to assess how the United States could assist other countries by sharing its agricultural expertise given that "insuring ample food for its people will be the number-one problem of most nations after this war is over."[2] The conference attendees were primarily U.S.-trained agricultural scientists, and they provided committee reports on the agricultural situation of eight regions of the world and separate "consultant" reports on various issues regarding extension efforts throughout the world. One of those consultants, Louise Stanley, who had been the head of the USDA's Bureau of Home Economics since 1923 and is listed at the conference as a special assistant to the research administrator at the USDA, wrote a short report outlining home demonstration work in the United States and how it might be useful elsewhere. Based on the American precedent, the "work should be organized under the leadership of a local homemaker who knows the needs and resources of the local community." The primary goals of such work should include the promotion of "better nutrition and healthful, satisfying conditions of living and so serve as an important factor in decreasing the high death rate of all groups," and the training of local leaders to take over the "important job of improving the conditions of home living and gear this group into an over-all national effort to build a level of living for the country based on its tradition and culture."[3] In other words, the goals were to educate local peoples about how to create better living conditions measured particularly in regard to health and nutritious food, and to train groups of people to take on these educational goals locally and nationally.

Both of these coincident events chart encounters between the USDA's extension service and U.S. philanthropic and governmental elites who were looking for models of how to enact postwar rural reconstruction. This chapter interrogates those encounters in order to understand what role (if any) the practices devised by Campbell and others at Tuskegee played in those postwar reconstruction efforts. As I have suggested throughout this book, the practices developed by Campbell, Daly, and other African Americans working for the USDA extension service within the Jim Crow South laid out a plan of action for how to improve rural living conditions for poor Black farmers within the constraints of structural racial and economic inequities. They conducted this plan by quietly and discretely attending to the sustaining of Black life, a form of resistance to the dispossessive and violent logics of plantation agriculture, with the belief that they were forging a future of racial and economic equity. By 1944, with officials in the United States and the United Kingdom considering how to improve rural conditions for people living overseas both as a geopolitical necessity (the promotion of democracy) and to fulfill the demands of global capital for new markets, resources, and laborers, the USDA's African

American extension service seemingly provided one model of action. Regarding the African survey, those officials represented American philanthropies and international missionary societies, in addition to officials at the U.K.'s Colonial Office, while those attending the conference in Washington, D.C. represented U.S. federal government agencies. Each of these groups was positioned to influence postwar policies overseas, and each considered—either directly in the case of the survey or indirectly in the case of the conference—the practices of the Black extension service as a model for those policies. The fact that Campbell was chosen to co-direct the African survey attests to the importance of his experiences in shaping what some policymakers were already calling development, while those involved in the 1944 and subsequent conferences looked to the extension service's work in the U.S. South, including its African American division, as providing an analogue to overseas rural reconstruction.

Through an analysis of the historical geographies of these two encounters, this chapter reveals how and why some aspects of the Black extension service served as models for postwar reconstruction. Unsurprisingly what this history reveals is that the practices of Campbell, Daly, and others that were in accord with the goals of liberal development—that is, aided self-help—were carried forward into the postwar period while the practices whose goals were more radical—such as home and land ownership—were not. What I show is that U.S. and U.K. elites who were planning for postwar rural reconstruction found useful models in some of the practices of Black extension work, particularly those that attended to the health and welfare of racialized peoples, while ignoring or overlooking practices that would have challenged the status quo. Put another way, and in accord with Bledsoe's and Wright's analyses of the foundational relationship between global capitalism and anti-Black racism, capitalist accumulation required the presence and labor of Black subjects—hence the attention to health and living conditions of rural peoples—while at the same time denying any spatial or historical agency to those subjects in the form of land ownership and a fundamental reordering of land tenure arrangements.[4]

## African American Education, the Phelps-Stokes Fund Surveys, and Thomas Campbell in Africa

Though distinctive in many ways that I will explore later, the 1944–945 survey was in actuality the third in a series of similar (though not identical) surveys, the first two of which focused on surveying educational facilities in Africa. In order to understand why Campbell was chosen to co-direct the 1944–1945 survey it is necessary to analyze the motivations behind these previous ones, particularly what they reveal about white elites' notions of education for African Americans and Africans. As many scholars have elucidated, the issue of who and how higher education would be provided for African Americans from emancipation onward—particularly in the South—was, to say the least, a contentious one.[5] Underlying these contentions in the late nineteenth and early twentieth centuries were disagreements over the future role of African Americans in U.S. society, with many white elites assuming that African Americans would continue to form the primary industrial workforce in the United States. For those elites, education was to be focused on practical matters that is, African Americans should be trained for jobs in industry and agriculture. Thomas Jesse Jones, a sociologist educated at Columbia, was the leading spokesperson for what became this dominant view of Black education. His first appointment in 1902, as head of research and sociology at Hampton Institute,[6] exposed him firsthand to the educational philosophy and practices of a facility whose goals were to train African Americans for the limited roles they were to play in society—as industrial and agricultural workers.[7] In 1910, Jones was appointed the head of the "negro section" of the U.S. census, and in 1913 became the educational director of the Phelps-Stokes Fund, a philanthropic organization with deep ties to both Tuskegee and Hampton Institutes.[8]

Jones was able to fully voice his views on practical education for African Americans in his book *Negro Education: A Study of the Private and Higher Schools for Colored People in the United States*, a publication that reported on the survey he had conducted of higher educational facilities for African Americans in the United States. The survey, initiated and supported by the General Education Board, was meant as a first step in promoting the development of state-funded education for African Americans,[9] but under Jones's influence became instead a vehicle for arguing for what he called an "education that will fit him [the African American] to undertake the responsibilities of life in the twentieth century."[10] Influenced by Progressive-era ideals, Jones strongly believed that education was key to shaping the next generation of "modern" citizens. Education, therefore, could not be imposed from a template drawn from classical learning, but instead had to be adapted "to the needs of the pupil and the community."[11] And given Jones's views of African Americans ("no racial group in the United States offers so many problems of economic and social adjustment as the ten million Negroes"[12]), those needs included far more than training for jobs. The aim of industrial education, Jones argues, "has always been the development of manhood and womanhood, through the common tasks of the common day."[13] What Jones was promoting, therefore, was a view of education that was far broader than either classical liberal arts or industrial training; it was meant to help solve the "problems of economic and social adjustment." An education that focused on the development of "manhood and womanhood" required attention to "correct" gender roles, family structure, work habits, character, and so forth and attention to industrial and agricultural training. These two aspects of education for African Americans that were key to Jones's philosophy—practical training, *and* character and community-building—became hallmarks of the educational policies supported by the Phelps-Stokes Fund in its work on Black education within the United States and its educational policies in Africa.

Like many prominent educators and leaders in the United States, Jones believed that the U.S. South could serve as an analogue for understanding race and race relations in other parts of the world. This form of Pan-Africanism—what King and others have called colonial Pan-Africanism[14]—differed from that espoused by Du Bois and others who looked to forms of African unity to counter racism and colonialism.[15] Jones viewed what he considered the successful U.S. experience of African American education, experiences that included the biopolitical practices of the USDA, as a template for managing colonial relations elsewhere. This more robust version of a colonial Pan-Africanism became evident in the interwar period, when the Phelps-Stokes Foundation commissioned a series of surveys of educational facilities in Africa, with Jones at the helm.

The first of those surveys was completed in 1922 and focused on West Africa; the second, in 1925, focused on East Africa.[16] Both of Jones's book-length reports following the surveys elaborated on his views that education for "natives" should be focused on practical skills, particularly agricultural and industrial, but that those skills could not be fully developed without attention to other issues of a more individual, familial, and communal nature. In the first report Jones emphasized the importance of education aimed at better health and home conditions. Health and hygiene, he suggests, "is among the very first responsibilities of the school and the teacher"[17] and a health program "should be included in every department of the school system."[18] Preparation for home life, Jones argues, is so crucial to "human society" that it shouldn't be relegated only to girls and domestic science but instead schools should plan "to make use of every school activity for the training of the youth in the essentials of home life."[19] Given what he considers the influence of women in these matters ("they control the character of the home and the training of the children"[20]), Jones offers advice about the importance of education for girls in Africa, thus portending what would later become a staple indicator of liberal forms of development.[21] Jones draws attention not only to the education of individuals but also to the rural community. Here he leaves little doubt about the influence of the USDA's practices among African-Americans: "Probably the most unique form of community education in rural districts is the 'Movable School' used so effectively by Tuskegee Institute in carrying the influence of that great institution among American Negroes of the rural district. . . . The following quotations present the essential elements of the school as they have appeared to competent observers."[22] The lengthy quotation that follows (seven paragraphs), Jones says, is derived "chiefly from a statement furnished by Mrs. A. W. Wilkie, of Gold Coast, Africa."[23]

In order to conduct this 1922 survey of West Africa, the directors of the Phelps-Stokes Foundation needed at least the tacit approval of the governments who controlled the area. To gain that approval, Jones visited and met with colonial officials in England, France, Belgium, and Portugal in early 1920.[24] And although many of these officials were initially skeptical of having a group of Americans "go through their colonies and look into whatever they wish,"[25] they all agreed to assist him. At the British Colonial Office (CO) that skepticism disappeared after Jones's 1922 report was published. The CO was "enthusiastic" about his written report, and "arranged for all of the educational officers in all of their colonies covered in the report to secure copies."[26]

The subsequent survey that focused on East African educational facilities, conducted in 1924, was initiated on the suggestion of the British Colonial Office, and included on its team of experts a prominent British colonial adviser, Hanns Vischer, secretary of the CO's Advisory Committee on Native Education in Tropical Africa[27] (fig. 5.1). Thus, it is apparent that British colonial experts found Jones's views of education particularly promising for colonial governance. The 1925 report provided recommendations similar to the 1922 report as it promoted educational adaptations in order to improve the "welfare of the African community."[28] Jones opens his 1925 report with a summary of what his team believed should be the major objectives of education in East Africa, objectives almost identical to those of the earlier report, with the addition of "character development," which he prioritizes by listing it as the first objective. "Government, missions and settlers were ready to agree that the development of character is a vital requisite in all educational activities," Jones argues, while "health as a second objective was recognized with equal unanimity."[29] Agricultural and industrial training, improving home life ("the care of children, food, sleeping facilities, sanitation and all that centers about the life of woman"[30]), and teaching "healthful recreations"[31] filled out that list.

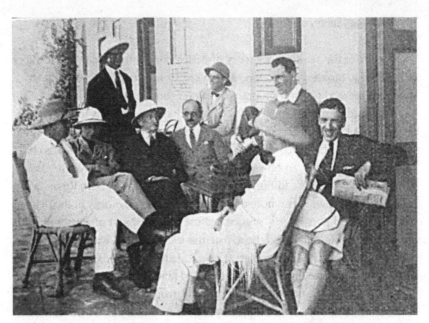

**FIGURE 5.1.** The East African Educational Commission, 1924, with Jones in the middle (without the hat). "The Phelps-Stokes Fund," by L. Hollingsworth Wood. Reprinted from *Opportunity, Journal of Negro Life*, October 1932, pp. 312–14, 322. Phelps-Stokes Collection, Schomburg Center for Research in Black Culture, New York City.

Jones makes clear why education in Africa should focus on these objectives (character development, health, agriculture and industrial skill, improvement of family life, and sound and healthful recreation). Labor, he argues, is needed to tap African physical resources, and skills alone without the management of these other, more social, aspects of peoples' lives, will not produce a good workforce. For example, after noting the high death rates in several areas of Africa, he suggests why colonial powers need to pay greater attention to health education: "Under such conditions the importance of education in matters of health becomes imperative. Even from the point of view of labor requirements in Colonial Africa, the present waste of Native life is almost disastrous to any adequate development of the resources. Under the stimulus and direction of industrial and agricultural organization, the demand for labor is increasing with great rapidity."[32] What was needed in Africa, he suggests, was an education not in the classical sense of training the mind, and not only for industrial/agricultural training, but in the "modern" sense of creating and maintaining a healthy (both in the physical sense and in the "moral" sense) workforce.

## The 1944–1945 Survey of Africa

The report of the 1944–1945 survey of Africa conducted under the auspices of the Phelps-Stokes Foundation reinforces this idea that education in Africa should be focused not only on practical matters but also on the goal of creating an "improved" population and reflects a trip that more directly links that education to the USDA's interventions in the U.S. South through the appointment of Thomas Campbell as co-director. As I suggested at the opening of this chapter, Campbell was not an obvious choice to co-direct the survey. The person who first suggested the addition of an African American—Emory Ross—was a missionary who had spent more than a decade in Africa, mostly in the Belgian Congo, and had persuasively argued against the worst sort of abuses of colonialism. He was familiar with the role of missions in Africa, was a firm believer that missionaries could provide great help in "education and development" of Africa,[33] and believed, like many in the United States and the United Kingdom, that having an African American on the trip would be beneficial since their "natural" links to Africa would predispose them to understand the culture in a more authentic manner. "An outstanding American Negro personality," he wrote to Jackson Davis, should be "added to the proposed field group."[34]

Ross's initial suggestion of John M. Ellison seemed a good one. Ellison was a highly educated and religious man, with a Ph.D. in Christian education from Drew University, and was serving as the first Black president of Virginia Union University. His training and experience in Christian education must have appealed to Ross, though he had no connection to Africa other than being an African American. Jackson Davis does not explicitly say why he chose Thomas Campbell over Ellison, although the fact that he knew Campbell personally through his many trips to Tuskegee as head of the General Education Board and was familiar with Campbell's work supervising the USDA's Black extension service, provides an important context for understanding his decision. Davis was well acquainted with Campbell's long history of working with poor Black tenant farmers and sharecroppers, his belief in the uplift of African Americans, and his educational philosophy. In a letter to Reuben Brigham, assistant director of the extension service, explaining why Campbell should be granted leave from the USDA to participate in the survey, Davis explains, "I feel that it would be essential to have an American Negro on the staff, and Mr. Campbell represents precisely the experience, the interest and the point of view which would be of greatest value in this inquiry."[35] The Colonial Office agreed that Campbell was a good choice, with Ross characterizing the invitation from London as "a warm one."[36] And apparently even U.S. State Department officials were interested in Campbell's insights as a Black man in Africa. While trying to expedite the issuance of Campbell's passport, Ross wrote to State Department officials, "Mr. Campbell's contribution in such a survey, and in the broader prospects of better Anglo-American-African understandings, we believe will be invaluable."[37]

According to Davis, Campbell's presence on the survey was indeed invaluable. Drawing on racist stereotypes, Davis explains that Campbell was able to connect with local people because of his personality and his southern rural experiences using song and other nonliterary devices to communicate. Davis writes from Brazil on route to Africa that "Campbell has made friends everywhere. You should see him 'talking' to these farm people. His sign language is irresistible."[38] In December from the Belgian Congo Davis writes that "Campbell made a great hit with his talks and singing."[39] What we know of his other contributions can be ascertained in a letter from Walter Schutz, head of a mission in Freetown, Sierra Leone, who writes to Davis to thank him and more particularly Campbell for visiting and inspiring the local people to work toward more self-improvement:

> The people who met you were happy for the privilege and you possibly did more good than you know. If our people here will be able to grasp the idea that they can do a lot for themselves if they put themselves to it, it will be a new day. Mr. Campbell and you helped us out there, I am sure. The things that were said at Battenburg Hall by Mr. Campbell sank rather deep. Coming from a man who is doing just that sort of thing, it was an eye opener to some of the people. I only wish you could have gone to a great many stations up country and talked to the people there.[40]

The few photos that exist of the trip depict Campbell surrounded by youth of different ages, informally posed for the camera (figs. 5.2, 5.3). Campbell, then, was serving precisely the role that Ross, Davis, and others had planned: as a Black man, he "naturally" could communicate with African people, and as someone who had done "just that sort of thing" in the U.S. South, he could inspire Africans to "do a lot for themselves if they put themselves to it."

That doctrine of self-help and the biopolitical metric of "improving" a population was reflected in the text of the report of the survey. As Davis, Campbell, andCed Wrong write in the introductory chapter of *Africa Advancing*, "Increasingly, European colonial powers realize that the development of Africa . . . can be accomplished only through the development of the people."[41]

**FIGURE 5.2.** Thomas Campbell surrounded by children. Original caption: "Campbell with African children." Campbell Collection, Tuskegee University Archives, Tuskegee University.

**FIGURE 5.3.** Thomas Campbell with unidentified group in Africa. Campbell Collection, Tuskegee University Archives, Tuskegee University.

Educational facilities, they suggest, should be focused not only on industrial and agricultural training, but also on what Jones had outlined in his earlier surveys—health, sanitation, family, and community, with a focus on communal self-help. In Liberia, for example, they suggest that "the schools can be more effective and supplement in many ways the program of the health department. Extension teachers now at work in agriculture may suggest the use of both men and women in similar services for work among the adult people in their homes, churches, and community gatherings in stimulating community effort to solve the problems of health, sanitation, and a better living."[42] A key chapter in the book with the telling title "Higher Standard of Life" makes the same point more generally, addressing what should be done to raise those standards since "efforts to increase production of farm crops does not necessarily result in better living for the persons who produce them."[43]

The "higher standard of living" that was being promoted throughout the book makes clear that the authors were already viewing Africa through a postwar lens, hoping to guide African elites not necessarily toward independence but, as they write, to help "Africans look forward to a progressive movement towards self-government."[44] In late 1944, when Davis, Campbell, and Wrong arrived in Africa, the Allied Forces had pushed the Axis powers into Italy, and colonial governments were reassessing the status of their "possessions." The opening sentences of *Africa Advancing* make clear the significance of the trip vis-à-vis the international context of 1944: "Probably nothing in the present disturbed international situation has more potentialities for good or ill than the development of the so-called backward or dependent peoples of the world and their adjustment to western civilization. Of all the great areas in the world, Africa has remained the most isolated and least developed."[45] The authors are giving voice to what was a dominant U.S. geopolitical stance at the time, that is, the status of what would come to be called the developing world was critical to geopolitical stability, and Africa as the "least developed" was surely central to that stability. As Jackson Davis put it in a letter to Brigham regarding the importance of having Campbell on the trip, "He would have an opportunity to render service of unusual significance to several African countries in determining policies and plans at a time when the situation is flexible."[46]

For the United Kingdom that flexible situation in Africa was fraught with complexity and importance. Its economic and cultural investment in the fate of its African colonies was growing rapidly, and its experts at the Colonial Office were in the process of modifying their views on the value of their colonial possessions. Increasingly wary of economic and ecological disruptions from the Great Depression and war, and fearing malnutrition and overpopulation in their African colonies, officials in the Colonial Office began to shift their focus from considering their colonies only as sites for the production of export commodities to recognizing that the local populations who labored to produce those commodities were under stress.[47] Colonial officials, wary of the crises that could ensue, began planning for expert interventions to improve the health of "native" populations.[48] Colonial administrators assumed that Africa would remain agricultural, but with a shift from primarily commercial to a more mixed form of agriculture, one that sustained the population and produced surplus. Such a shift required new agricultural schemes and different educational requirements. Experts at the Colonial Office therefore realized that they needed new knowledge of each colony and its ecological and economic situation in order to better reform systems of production and reproduction.[49] "What was needed was a comprehensive program of rural reconstruction and community betterment," Hodge suggests, "one that would demand the close integration of education policy with economic development planning, on a colony-wide basis, and the coordination and cooperation of all the different agencies responsible for social welfare work, especially the Church and missions."[50] Surveys of educational facilities—like the one undertaken by Davis, Campbell, and Wrong—were to be encouraged.

*Africa Advancing* includes a chapter devoted to what the authors call "new colonial policies" in which they make the case that to ready British colonies in Africa for self-government, their economies should be made more self-sufficient. Davis, Campbell, and Wrong contend that colonial agriculture must shift from an emphasis on plantation-style, export commodities to a more diversified agricultural base in order to produce a more consistent supply of food. They argued that creating a stable and manageable colonial population that can take care of its own biological needs—food, health care, and so forth—should become the focus for adult education. Their description of new British colonial policies included an emphasis on mass literacy, while for adults, "the state [should] bring to the people all knowledge useful for dealing with their problems of home, farm and community life, including the best use of their resources, the production and preparation of food, and the improvement of public health."[51] In other words, the authors are promoting what Hodge, Hödl, and Kopf refer to as the "human side of colonial development," that is, attempting to manage a population through raising its standards of living.[52] This is made clear in their concluding chapter, where they offer suggestions for the improvement of educational facilities in Africa based on their assumptions that "the development of the country depends on the development of the African population."[53] And that development, they argue, involves "concurrent advance in health, standard of life, commercial and agricultural improvement, and political responsibility."[54] But that political responsibility was not assumed to lead to independence: "It is clear that African territories are advancing wherever African peoples and European powers work together. They need each other."[55]

At the suggestion of the Colonial Office, Davis and Campbell returned to the United States via England and Scotland and visited with prominent British colonial and missionary officials in London and Edinburgh. With postwar geopolitics already under consideration, the fate of Africa—its "potentialities for good or ill"—was of paramount concern.[56] Accompanied by Thomas Jesse Jones, they traveled to Washington, D.C., where they met with USDA officials.[57] The official photographs of Campbell with the secretary of Agriculture, Claude Wickard, suggest the new envisioning of the postwar order that was already underway in the offices in Washington, D.C., as Campbell is posed pointing on a map and globe to the areas of Africa just visited (figs. 5.4, 5.5). And the title of the article in *Newspic* reporting on this meeting—"Light Is Coming to the Dark Continent"—draws on a long-standing racist trope of civilization and development, and points to the intent of U.S. postwar interventions in Africa.[58] Soon after returning to New York, Davis met with Robert Lester of the Carnegie Corporation to discuss his trip and to make future plans for American experts to travel to Africa. In his summary of the conversation, Davis writes, "Africa, especially in British territories, is on the eve of great extensions of educational opportunity, and there is keen interest in a utilization of our experiences in the South with extension services and community type of education."[59]

Davis and Campbell worked quickly with Wrong to complete the book manuscript that was published as *Africa Advancing* in the fall of 1945. The book was distributed not only to experts at the Colonial Office and through the network of the International Missionary Councils but also to the heads of agricultural extension and departments of education in the southern states so that they could appreciate the connection between African and African American education.[60] In his letter to the various agencies of the Foreign Missions Conference of North America about the forthcoming publication of *Africa Advancing*, Emory Ross suggests that the book should have global appeal. "The report," he writes, "is of especial interest to missions and educators in all part[s] of Africa. But there is in it material of significance for others parts of the world where rural populations predominate, where illiteracy is widespread, where general education with regard to land and its uses is desirable, and where problems of mass education face governments and missions."[61]

**FIGURE 5.4.** Thomas Campbell and Secretary of Agriculture Claude Wickard posed around a map of Africa. Original caption: "Shows Campbell returning from Africa in 1945 pointing to areas visited for the general education board." Campbell Collection, Tuskegee University Archives, Tuskegee University.

**FIGURE 5.5.** Thomas Campbell and Secretary of Agriculture Claude Wickard posed around a globe. Original caption: "T. M. Campbell, left, Extension Service field agent of the USDA, points out to Secretary Claude R. Wickard some of the regions of West Africa where a chain of movable schools could be established. Campbell has just returned from a six-month education survey of West Africa with an Anglo-American mission." *Newspic*, June 1945. Campbell Collection, Tuskegee University Archives, Tuskegee University.

With the report now in the hands of white U.S. elites—philanthropists, missionaries, government officials—its insights could be used to shape postwar U.S. policies in what became known as the developing world. Campbell returned to Tuskegee and picked up his work just where he had left it; trying to assist Black farmers through attention to health, sanitation, and home and land ownership.

## The 1944 Conference

When Wilson addressed the opening of the 1944 Contribution of Extension Methods and Techniques Toward the Rehabilitation of War-Torn Countries Conference, he too spoke of how best to provide education to rural farmers. Science, he wrote in his opening address, was applicable not only to the technical aspects of agriculture, but also to what he termed the social scientific aspects: "marketing, farm management, land tenure, cooperative organizations, recreation, rural schools and education."[62] And by addressing these needs, extension work, he argues, not only improves the standard of living, but also contributes to democracy. Here Wilson anticipates some of the uncertainties of the postwar era: "Those who take part in extension work are being rewarded by being able to enjoy a better living and by realizing to the fullest the opportunities of democratic citizenship."[63] Extension work is required, Wilson argued, to transform certain groups of people by raising their standard of living, thus ensuring democracy around the world.

At the close of the conference, Edmund Brunner, a rural sociologist with a long history of working with the federal government on agricultural issues, summarized what had been accomplished and how to move forward. In so doing, he specifies what he calls rural similarities that characterize the peoples of the world who need extension work: They "practice a hoe agriculture, not horsepower but human brawn produces their crops. Their holdings are small, their families large. Their diet is bare, their land often the property of others.... They share the problem of rearing and educating half their children . . . of achieving for themselves some degree of social and economic parity with other elements of society or, if you prefer, of establishing for themselves those freedoms the leaders of the great democracies declare to be essential for the enduring peace of the world."[64] And these people in need of rehabilitation, Brunner argues, are to be found not only overseas, but in the United States as well. "Extension work is for all," Brunner says, "yet groups, even classes, do exist in many societies. The large landowner has no more claim on extension than does the small tenant, though the needs will differ, as will the educational approach in meeting those needs. I am thinking here, for instance, not only of the rubber and tea plantations of the tropics, but of the cotton plantations of our own South. Let us not forget, we who are Americans, that, as already stated, we have similarities to other countries among our own disadvantaged groups on the land."[65] Here Brunner says what must have been obvious to many at the conference: those who are really in need of extension work are particular groups of people, or "classes," similar to tenant farmers in the Cotton Belt of the U.S. South. Race is never explicitly mentioned in the report, but Brunner certainly implies its meaning here.

Just as Thomas Jesse Jones and other U.S. elites considered the U.S. South and its problems as an analogue for analyzing African problems, Brunner and others working with federal agencies who were familiar with the extension service in the U.S. South looked to it for solutions to global rural problems in places where classes of people were trying to achieve "for themselves some degree of social and economic parity with other elements of society" and to establish "for themselves those freedoms the leaders of the great democracies declare to be essential for the enduring peace of the world." This 1944 conference then, begins to formalize and put into institutional channels the ways in which the USDA's extension work, particularly in the U.S. South and particularly regarding its "classes," can be applied globally. Although overshadowed in history by the conference that preceded it by two months—the United Nations Monetary and Financial Conference, otherwise known as the Bretton Woods Conference, held in New Hampshire in July of 1944—this USDA conference was also critical for establishing postwar U.S. hegemony.

Like Bretton Woods, the Contribution of Extension Methods and Techniques Toward the Rehabilitation of War-Torn Countries Conference represented the culmination of years of discussion and debate. Wilson had spent the early 1940s planning for the extension service to play a key role in postwar reconstruction. In 1942, he organized what he referred to as "informal discussions" with Leslie A. Wheeler, the director of the Office of Foreign Agricultural Relations (at this time part of the USDA), and other prominent Washington, D.C. insiders as part of a series of discussions that were held at the Cosmos Club. The subject of these discussions was "food, agriculture, and improvement of world nutrition," and the six-page note Wilson wrote to initiate these discussions lays out an agenda for "a possible United Nations Approach to Economic Reconstruction." His opening sentences make clear that for Wilson economic reconstruction meant biopolitical interventions. "Food," he writes, "is the most essential of all human needs while the conditions of those engaged in agriculture is the greatest social problem of the world. Hence a joint attack upon the problems of health and agriculture should do more to increase world health and happiness and to improve economic conditions than any other single form of economic action."[66] These initiatives might have positioned Wilson to take charge of postwar planning for rural reconstruction, but that was not to be the case. Instead, President Roosevelt circumvented the USDA, convening a United Nations conference on food and agriculture in 1943 that led to the formation of the Food and Agriculture Organization of the United Nations (FAO), the agency charged with oversight of international efforts to combat hunger.

Nonetheless, Wilson continued to believe that the extension service was best situated to provide postwar relief and he pushed forward his agenda of using his agency as a platform for reconstruction efforts. In a 1947 letter, he suggested that while the FAO was still caught up with internal organizational matters, the extension service is "due for rapid growth throughout the world, particularly if we are to have a peaceful world in which the standard of living is rapidly increasing."[67] Two years later, Wilson organized a follow-up conference, this one titled Extension Experiences Around the World, with goals similar to its 1944 predecessor. The opening address, delivered by an assistant to the secretary of agriculture, William A. Minor, made explicit mention of Truman's inaugural address: "In recent months much discussion has been centered on the President's Point 4 Program to extend technology and the benefits of science for improvement of underdeveloped areas of the world. This conference, therefore, would seem to be an early effort toward the implementation of the President's hope for other countries to receive the benefits of technology."[68] And that "implementation" was noticeable in the conference report as the discussion of national agricultural extension was transformed into the discourse of international rural reconstruction and development. The regions under discussion, for example, expanded from the 1944 conference to include Latin America and Africa, and the "problems" that were discussed were not voiced in the language of agricultural extension per se ("farm demonstration" and "home demonstration") but rather ranged more broadly and fluidly. The committee on Latin America, for example, divided its analysis into three main areas—farm, home, and community problems—with the latter two comprising the bulk of discussion (fifteen of the twenty main points). The committee on the Middle East likewise identified ten major problems, of which only two pertained directly to agriculture ("problem of monoculture" and "the application of modern techniques to agricultural production"). The other eight problems included population growth ("equally fundamental and important is the problem of population growth in relation to cultivated areas,"[69]), land distribution, tribal settlement, and health and sanitation problems. The committee on Africa reported "the trouble is that without better health, better food, better education, and new and socially acceptable incentives, natural resources cannot be exploited."[70] This sentiment clearly matches that put forward in *Africa Advancing*; raising the standard of living of Africans, in other words, was considered essential for their development. And the key to raising that standard were interventions aimed at teaching better home and health practices, interventions that had proved successful in the U.S. South, particularly those developed by Black home demonstration agents like Laura Daly: efforts aimed at food production, childcare, health care, and home improvements. As discussed in chapter 2, from the early 1920s on, white home demonstration work concentrated on home consumption, while Black home demonstrators reinforced their focus on food production and health care.

### And After

A decade later in 1959, the USDA's extension service published *Homemaking Around the World*, an introduction for women being trained as home economists who were going to work in the USDA's foreign extension service. The opening chapter informs these women that their jobs will require attention not only to the details of domestic work but also to the deeper principles of individual and family relations: "basic principles of bringing about any change in the living habits of a people and in their thinking; basic principles in human relations that govern a way of living; basic principles in the performance of small skills that may lead to larger practices."[71] The subject of each chapter and the order of their appearance indicate where those interventions would occur: childcare, food and nutrition, home management, health and sanitation, home gardens, poultry, rabbit and goat production, housing and home improvement, and care and the production of clothing. This book was reprinted throughout the 1960s and 1970s, when the new United States Agency for International Development added its sponsorship and name to the title page.

It was also joined in 1971 by a more detailed hands-on guide, *Homemaking Handbook*, meant, as the second half of its title indicated, for women "village workers in many countries." The opening chapter of the guide, titled "Village Women Help Build Nations" outlines the rationale for why U.S. experts in home economics are vital to development. The new housewife, the authors say, wants "better living for her family ... she thinks of plenty of good food, improved housing, and better health for her family, better care and education for her children."[72] With better living, they go on to say, nations are strengthened: "governments are beginning to recognize that helping the family and the home helps the nation. They recognize that good homes, happy families, and educated children are basic to a great nation."[73] This far more detailed and lengthier guide follows a similar chapter outline as the 1959 book with some small changes: food and nutrition, growing food at home, food storage and preservation, childcare, health, housing and home improvement, housekeeping and home management, and clothing. It also includes a lengthy section on teaching methods, beginning with the importance of finding and training local leaders to assist with the work.

Many of the descriptions of "village work in foreign countries" is similar—and at times identical—to descriptions of Black home demonstration work in the U.S. South; a similarity not only in terms of subject matter, but also in regard to pedagogical practices such as identifying local leaders, forming canning clubs, and using those leaders to demonstrate better techniques of health and home management. The introductory chapter of *Homemaking Around the World* refers to "the pioneer days of extension work in the United States," when a home demonstrator would learn how to be proficient in one skill first before moving on to others. Two of those skills are singled out for attention: "Sometimes it was the making of peanut butter from homegrown peanuts if there was little or no knowledge in rural areas about the process," the section begins, while "sometimes it was building a fireless cooker, for which there was great need at a time when farm women worked in the fields alongside their husbands, and there was little time for cooking."[74] The section continues with a discussion of how such skills will help solidify the importance of the home agent as they proceed in their overseas home extension work. As I've discussed in chapter 2, demonstrations regarding constructing and using the fireless cooker were integral to Black home demonstration work, while experiments with the various uses of peanuts was one of George Washington Carver's many contributions to botany. "Pioneering days," therefore, is clearly a reference to Black extension work, although this fact is never made explicit.

The *Homemaking Handbook* is well-illustrated with photographs taken, according to the preface, by staff of the Agency for International Development and the Food and Agriculture Organization—two of the sponsoring agencies—as well as UNICEF (United Nation Children's International Emergency Fund). Many bear similarities to images analyzed in this book; that is, they depict women agents demonstrating certain homemaking duties to

**FIGURE 5.6.** Women in India watching an infant being weighed. Original caption: "This Indian village worker helps the women check on the growth and development of their babies." *Homemaking Handbook*, Extension Service, U.S. Department of Agriculture in Cooperation with Agency for International Development, March 1981, p. 111

other, less-skilled, women. Somewhat uncannily, one photograph (fig. 5.6) is almost identical to figure 2.3: local women posing around the authority figure (either a local leader or a nurse or doctor) who is demonstrating how to correctly weigh infants. Note the similarity not only in the subject matter and pose, but also in the technologies assembled—a table brought outside covered in a white cloth, an infant being weighed using a tabletop, portable scale, and an authority figure with pencil in hand about to record the weight. The original title of figure 2.3— "Better Babies"—is a reference to a campaign established by the U.S. Children's Bureau to combat infant mortality in the first decades of the twentieth century that was popularized through a series of "better baby" contests held at state fairs. These contests produced a series of images and photographs similar to this one, with the figure of a medical professional depicted measuring and recording baby weight. By the late 1920s, when this photograph was taken, national "Better Baby" campaigns were on the wane as the idea of promoting better health was transformed and expanded by proponents of eugenics into creating "fitter families."[75] Also in the 1920s, as discussed in chapter 2, white home demonstration agents had switched their emphasis to home consumption, while Black home demonstration agents had amplified their efforts in regard to reducing infant mortality and supporting home health care, efforts that were expanded through the Great Depression. Thus, in the 1960s and 1970s when the USDA extension service and USAID were putting together these handbooks with attention to childcare in the "developing world," it was Black home demonstration work that provided the most direct model.

The uncanny visual similarity between these two figures, and the verbal references to "pioneering days of extension work," document the ways in which some of the practices of the Black extension service functioned as models for liberal development projects overseas. Practices of self-improvement aimed at fulfilling basic needs became the mantra of private philanthropies, missions, and U.S. government agencies that hoped through community interventions to "develop" and make more democratic overseas countries and cultures.[76] And as Thomas Campbell's presence on the 1944 survey attests, the direct experience of teaching people that "they can do a lot for themselves if they put themselves to it" positioned Black extension agents as potential development experts.[77] At the same time, the two encounters between the USDA extension service and the philanthropic and governmental elites of the United States and the United Kingdom that I've documented in this chapter suggest how other practices of Black extension work—particularly those aimed at home and land ownership that would end tenant and sharecropping arrangements—were not incorporated into most development planning nor into the schemes that constituted community development overseas.[78] And neither Laura Daly nor Thomas Campbell were ever called on to serve as development experts; instead their work at Tuskegee to help poor Black farmers continued unabated in the postwar period as they struggled against white plantation owners and landlords whose newly mechanized cotton fields pushed more and more Black farmers off the land.[79] The anti-Black racism that undergirded plantation agriculture in the U.S. South plagued community development schemes overseas, creating profits for innumerable agricultural, infrastructural, and industrial corporations through the exploitation and impoverishment of peoples and lands. Community development schemes failed, according to Immerwahr, because their planners overlooked power both "within communities and the larger societies around them,"[80] *and,* as I've tried to show in this book, because that power was and is sustained by racism that denies spatial and historical agency to non-white people.[81]

# CONCLUSION

In 1944, Laura Daly was appointed a field representative for the Consumer Division of the United States' Office of Price Administration (fig. 6.1).[1] The additional authority and power she must have gained from that position are evident in the few remnants we have of her later writings that are preserved in archives, writings that point to the on-going re-enactments of racist thought and practice in the United States. In 1962, she wrote on a postcard to James Meredith, a civil rights activist and the first Black student admitted to the University of Mississippi: "You must have felt as Jesus did when the mob was yelling 'crucify him! crucify him!' I hope you were able to pray as he did—saying 'Father, forgive them, for they know not what they do.' And we are praying for you."[2] And in 1965, she donated ninety dollars to Dr. Martin Luther King Jr.'s Southern Christian Leadership Conference, receiving a lengthy reply from King in which he thanks her for her generosity and talks of the escalating movement to exercise voting rights in Alabama; he ends the letter with his hopes for the future (hopes that fifty-seven years later have yet to be fulfilled): "The Civil Rights movement is striving to eradicate slums and those conditions which make for slums, by pressing for such goals as fairer job opportunities, increased minimum wage payments, and quality, integrated education and housing."[3] A woman who spent much of her career helping other women to become better housewives, and then later supported the goals of the civil rights movement, Daly's life spanned a generational shift from the ideology of uplift to the politics of protest.

And yet the politics of protest were not completely new to Daly. As an employee of the USDA's African American extension service for most of her life, Daly's enactments of uplift contained within them elements of dissent. Although her work at Tuskegee may not have led to large-scale structural changes, the USDA's and Tuskegee's efforts at uplifting Black sharecrop-

**FIGURE C.1.** Laura R. Daly as a field representative for the Office of Price Administration. United States Office for Emergency Management. Laura R. Daly, Field Representative, Consumer Division, Office of Price Administration OPA. United States [between 1940 and 1946].

pers and tenant farmers did have effects that challenged white supremacy. As I made clear in chapter 2, her job as a home demonstrator focused on sustaining Black life amid conditions that devalued it, a form of labor that Mullings has called "life-work." And this life-work contained its own liberatory potential, as it created "restorative spaces that provided economic and social resources needed to survive," and offered a means for people to "resist the dispossession of their bodies and souls."[4] In addition, a racist labor system had little tolerance for Black women found "idle" during planting or harvesting season, that is, not working in the fields. Yet as the many testimonials discussed in chapter 3 make clear, some women found it possible to join the ranks of "proper" housewives, assisted through Tuskegee's home demonstrators.[5] Moreover, the farmers who were able to purchase their own farms with assistance from Tuskegee and the USDA presented direct threats to plantation agriculture and the white landlords who relied on their devalued labor. Home and land ownership was its own form of resistance, a way of claiming one's own place in the world, a step toward what McKittrick has called a "Black sense of place."[6] And as a powerful place and institution, Tuskegee itself was a threat to white power. The people who worked and were educated there may not have conducted conscious acts of resistance, but some of them found within its spaces a livelihood, an education, a community, and a source of personal and political authority.

As this book has made clear, the politics of uplift as developed and practiced by people like Daly and Campbell working for the Black cooperative extension service was its own subtle form of resistance, a polite politics, that was neither noted nor meant to be noticed. With limited funding and staff, and in a time and place that constrained most efforts to improve Black rural lives, Campbell, Daly, and others were able to negotiate between the various mandates put before them in order to directly assist Black farm families living in the U.S. South. They did so by carefully and quietly shaping the USDA's directives to suit their own purposes. In each case, they did their best to implement rural improvement and uplift within a context of white supremacy that prevented those processes from wholly succeeding. Some practices they developed from scratch, like the movable school, while others were adapted and tweaked from what was handed down to them from Washington, D.C. As the previous chapters relate, throughout the course of the 1920s and 1930s, as white home demonstration work shifted to teaching women how to improve their skills as consumers, Black home demonstration work remained focused on fulfilling food and health needs, while New Deal resettlement schemes were quickly adapted by Campbell and others to achieve their long-standing interest in creating communities of Black landowners.

Black home demonstration work showed poor farm women improved ways to grow and prepare food, take care of their children, and produce clothing and other domestic goods, ensuring the survival of family and community. Staffed with a farm demonstrator, home demonstrator, and nurse, the movable school provided direct assistance to farm families in the form of agricultural training, demonstrations of food and clothing production, and professional health care. These forms of aided self-help were usually welcome by white landlords who relied on the labor of Black sharecroppers and tenant farmers; put another way, these practices did not—at least on the surface— threaten the plantation style of agriculture that characterized the Cotton Belt. Yet as I've tried to show throughout this book, even as these practices were welcome by landlords and lauded by the USDA, agents like Daly and Campbell saw their work as part of a larger effort to uplift their race, an effort they believed would gradually lead to racial equity and the undermining of the systemic devaluing of Black lives that sustained plantation agriculture. Embedded within the verbal and visual accounts of their work that I've examined here—official reports, photographs, Campbell's book, and the USDA film—and repeated for emphasis, were representations of the actions, narratives, and aesthetic of uplift. Local white elites could easily overlook any political significance in these enactments and representations of uplift. It is only in retrospect and taken cumulatively that their more radical nature can be seen. The goal of uplift—racial parity—was not the goal of the USDA, nor could it coexist with plantation agriculture. What Daly and Campbell were enacting, therefore, was different from their white counterparts, and its potential success presented a direct threat to white supremacy. But as I've noted in this book, that threat was kept muted; racial uplift by definition was meant as a gradual process and Black USDA agents rarely if ever articulated the political significance of its endpoint. Other practices of the Black extension service that were more explicitly political, such as Tuskegee's establishment of Black land-owning communities from the time of Washington onward that culminated in Prairie Farms, met with limited success. Local landlords and white elites were either indifferent to these arrangements, or as was the case with local Farm Security administrators, used their racist assumptions to criminalize the inhabitants and deem them unworthy as property-owning citizens.

Working within the many constraints posed by the Jim Crow South, these accomplishments in developing mechanisms to assist and sustain Black farmers' lives, thereby potentially undermining white supremacy, are remarkable in and of themselves. That they form an important, although forgotten, component in the complex historical geographies of international development is equally remarkable. Visitors to Tuskegee during this time—representatives of missionary agencies, philanthropists, social scientists—who came to witness uplift as actualized through the type of practical education it dispensed in its classrooms also learned about the USDA's cooperative extension service's rural improvements brought directly to farmhouses through its movable school and home demonstration work. Armed with knowledge of those improvements and the mechanisms for delivering them, those visitors then returned to their respective northern institutions where what they had learned at Tuskegee was adapted to suit the needs of governments and agencies seeking models of how to manage different and potentially "problematic" people. Throughout the 1930s and 1940s and particularly as World War II drew to a close, officials in the British Colonial Office understood the need to shift their colonial governance strategies, while government officials in Washington, D.C. began seeking models of how to manage a world in which improving the lives of rural, racialized people outside the United States played a critical role. As this book has made clear, some of the practices developed by the African American cooperative extension service of the USDA, particularly those whose aim was to provide better food and health care, offered one such model.

Taken out of the hands of agents like Daly and Campbell and therefore devoid of the political intent of uplift—racial parity—the practices of the African American extension service provided a model of how to improve rural farmers' lives, and hence provide a stable labor force, without disturbing the different forms of racial capitalism that the United States and the United Kingdom were practicing and imposing in their liberal development schemes around the world. These schemes were particularly useful in Britain's decolonization projects and in the United States' newly forged, "pointillist" empire.[7] What became known as community development in places like India, Southeast Asia, and portions of Africa—interventions scaled down to the local and with an ethos of aided self-help—explicitly drew on the model provided by Black home demonstration work as it had evolved in the 1920s and 1930s, without of course any intent to end racial or economic injustice. White, rural "experts"—sociologists, anthropologists, economists, geographers—filled the offices of emerging government development agencies and private institutes, bringing with them their training from elite universities and their understandings of "backward" societies. As scholars have noted,[8] the translation of academic knowledge into the practices of international development was neither a simple nor uncontested process, but what came to be called the development framework "excluded many questions that are quite germane to questions of poverty, power, and change."[9] Rather, it was defined by a knowledge that favored landlords over peasants, village "leaders" over farmers, men over women, and in general, sociospatial constraints over mobility.[10] Development experts overlooked structural inequities and were blind to their own racism and to its institutionalized, foundational role in maintaining those inequities. This means that not only was the agency of Black people overlooked, but that the political intent of uplift as practiced by Black USDA agents like Daly and Campbell went missing.

By countering this white washing of the story of the USDA's extension service and its shaping of community development overseas, this book has implications beyond the particularities of Black federal employees in the Jim Crow South. First, documenting the lives, words, and actions of people like Daly and Campbell highlights a hitherto fore unknown episode in the long history of Black struggle against racial capitalism in the United States, showing in particular how those struggles can succeed even within structures (institutional and societal) that were overwhelmingly oppressive. As chapters 2, 3, and

4 have shown, agents like Laura Daly and Thomas Campbell devised mechanisms to resist the anti-Black racism that sustained plantation agriculture, mechanisms that drew on the ideology and aesthetics of uplift. Even as they were constrained by a system of white supremacy and the systemic diminishment of Black lives that characterized plantation agriculture, they showed how this form of racial capitalism could be quietly and subtly resisted. As I've detailed in this book, the African American extension service's Home Demonstration Unit and movable school assisted the life-work of social reproduction that enabled the continuation of Black forms of survival on and with the land, sustaining practices and knowledges that were their own forms of resistance, as well as necessary steps toward land ownership and racial and economic equity.[11] That this story has gone unremarked has denied to history, and therefore to those searching for precedent, the remarkable, complicated, and significant story of how people can struggle within, sometimes along, and quietly against, the constraints of racial capitalism. The narratives of agents like Daly and Campbell, therefore, provide vivid cases of how, in McKittrick and Woods's words, "the lives of subaltern subjects are shaped by, and are shaping, the imaginative, three-dimensional, social, and political contours of human geographies." Working "within and against the grain of dominant modes of power, knowledge, and space," the narratives and lived experiences of Daly and Campbell, McKittrick, and Woods argue, "need to be taken seriously."[12]

Second, by examining how some of the practices devised by Daly and Campbell served as models for community development projects overseas, it makes explicit the ways in which the devaluing of Black lives that was foundational to plantation agriculture persisted into the postwar period. As chapter 5 details, the community development ethos of guided self-help through neverending rounds of hard work, an ethos geared toward maintaining a healthy, racialized, labor force that was always "undeveloped," is rooted in the logic of the plantation. At the same time, given that this book has also exposed the resistance that was embedded in the ideology of uplift as expressed through the Black USDA extension service, it provides an important case study for understanding how other people, living under their own constraints of racial capitalism, have resisted and continue to resist those limitations. The mechanisms devised by agents like Daly and Campbell were not the loud, bellicose, bloody protests that make headlines and that leave explicit marks in the archives; the protests, in other words, that are more commonly written about in history books. Instead, they were quiet, subtle, everyday acts undertaken by relatively minor actors in situations that have been overlooked by scholars. Drawing attention to these acts of resistance as they operated in the U.S. South under conditions of plantation agriculture should go a long way to understanding similar acts of quiet resistance within other schemes of liberal development.

Ernest Neal, one of the first Black employees of the U.S. Agency for International Development (USAID) whose training included work with Black resettlement communities during the New Deal, reflected on his time spent overseeing community development projects in India, the Philippines, Liberia, and Sierra Leone: "The concept that villages could be developed largely through aided self-help was too simplistic to cope with the magnitude and complexity of modernizing village societies." Neal's lament about the failure of aided self-help—the mantra of the USDA's extension service—in "alleviating social injustices that accounted for much of the poverty in villages such as tenancy, usurious credit and marketing" may well echo the frustrations and constraints faced by people like Thomas Campbell and Laura Daly.[13] After a lifetime of working on community development projects around the world, Neal understood the many limitations of liberal development schemes and their failure to confront the root causes of poverty. His own personal search for those causes—to the facts of social and economic injustice—may well have been shaped by his experiences before he began his career at USAID, when he worked with New Deal resettlement communities and then just after the war, at Tuskegee.

It's possible that Laura Daly met Ernest Neal during those postwar years when he was based at Tuskegee overseeing the Rural Life Council, an initiative to improve rural living conditions in the areas surrounding Tuskegee that was funded by the General Education Board.[14] If so, she probably followed his career as he secured his position with USAID and headed overseas, first to India. One can only imagine what she would have thought if she had seen her work in rural Alabama being replicated in rural India, disembedded from its politics of racial and economic justice—and then Liberia, Sierra Leone, and the Philippines—with effects as mixed as her own. She might have been struck, like I was, with the similarities between the description from *Homemaking Handbook* of a Mrs. Hudan, a woman who became a model "village leader," and Mrs. Jamerson, the woman who "can Can" (see fig. 2.8). Mrs. Hudan, the guide explains,

> grows beautiful tomatoes, but no one else in the village has much success with tomatoes. The other women in the club want to learn how Mrs. Hudan grows tomatoes. She was asked to tell the club what she did. She was timid at first. The village worker helped Mrs. Hudan demonstrate each step. The vil-

lage worker taught Mrs. Hudan more about tomatoes and helped her prepare for each demonstration. Mrs. Hudan has experience, knowledge, and ability in growing tomatoes. As the village worker trained and helped her, she gained more confidence in herself. Soon she was trying out new vegetables and talking to the club about the need for good gardens. Mrs. Hudan developed into a garden leader in the village.[15]

Like Mrs. Hudan, Mrs. Jamerson had clearly been singled out as a leader in the community. Her 1928 photograph speaks of her pride in her accomplishments and her "confidence in herself." It also—through its refusal to participate in the aesthetics of uplift—suggests a defiance. According to the dictates of uplift aesthetics, Mrs. Jamerson should be depicted actively engaged in the work of self-help, canning her produce. Instead, she is facing the camera head-on, looking at us. She is refusing the movement of work that defined the gradual process of uplift and rural improvement, and instead is facing the camera in a way that suggests a direct and immediate confrontation with injustice.

This photograph is one of the few representations in the archive of the Black extension service that suggests not the polite politics of gradual uplift but a more immediate resistance. It's a poignant reminder of what was at stake in that polite politics, and that is a belief that with time and a lot of work—through the process of racial uplift—racial justice would be achieved. As a village leader, Mrs. Hudan may have taken to her new work with a sense of personal or collective politics whose success would be measured in structural changes to social and economic regimes. We can never know. But what we do know is that the white women from the United States who "trained and helped her" did not share that politics. Emptied of its more radical intent of racial and economic justice, home demonstration work certainly assisted some women in dealing with their impossible situation of serving as laborers and housewives, but it did not contain an imagined future of racial equity. The transformation of Mrs. Hudan from timid to confident was meant to demonstrate how hard work and training—aided self-help—could bring about better food and therefore a healthier workforce, not a more just economic system.

But the unknown history of Mrs. Hudan's life opens possibilities for imagining otherwise. Her success at gardening no doubt contributed to the sustenance of her family and community, thereby creating value that could not be appropriated by local landowners or global agricultural corporations. This form of life-work, like the many food preparation, gardening, and health care demonstrations conducted by Laura Daly and Luella Hanna, contained its own liberatory potential. Perhaps she was participating in home demonstration work because she believed in a form of polite politics, planning on using what she had learned to eventually attain equity for herself and her community.[16] Or perhaps she simply was biding her time in productive work until she could directly confront the systemic devaluing of her life and livelihood. Perhaps, in other words, she was connected to Laura Daly and Mrs. Jamerson in ways far more profound than growing tomatoes.

Laura Daly, Thomas Campbell, and the many other agents of the USDA's Black extension service labored daily to find ways of countering the degradations and injustices of living in the Jim Crow South through their work with the USDA. Their many accomplishments—their everyday work to assist Black farmers made possible through their quiet disregard of some USDA mandates and their "noisy" (because repeated and represented) regard for other mandates, and through their long-term goals of racial uplift that were actualized in plans for Black home and land-owning communities—demonstrate what can be achieved through collective agency in the form of a polite politics, as well as what required more direct action.

# NOTES

**CHAPTER 1. Laura R. Daly and the United States Department of Agriculture**

1. Laura R. Daly, "Annual Report of Home Demonstration Work for Women and Girls, Calendar Year 1919," ACES (Alabama Cooperative Extension Service) Collection, box 107, Special Collections and Archives, Auburn University Libraries.

2. Robert Francis Engs, *Educating the Disfranchised and Disinherited: Samuel Chapman Armstrong and Hampton Institute, 1839–1893* (Knoxville: University of Tennessee Press, 1999).

3. Laura Blanche Randolph Daly first came to my attention as I was sifting through Auburn University's ACES archival collection in the early days of working on this project. I was drawn to a set of annual reports from the Home Demonstration Unit that were comprehensive, easy to read, and that contained rather lengthy descriptions in the narrative sections that allowed the author to write freely. I investigated further and realized that these reports were written by Daly. As I continued my research at Auburn and at the archives at Tuskegee University, her name appeared repeatedly on reports, in letters, and in descriptions from outside visitors to Tuskegee. I became very curious about her life, and from online searching found several photos of her and identified her as the primary subject of the 1928 set of photographs taken by a USDA official to document the work of the Home Demonstration Unit of the African American extension service. I was able to locate and talk with Barbara Lawler (Daly's daughter, Mildred Daly Maxwell, was Barbara's godmother), who shared with me many stories about Laura Daly's personal and professional life and showed me her 1906 diploma from Hampton Institute and photographs of her from different periods of her life.

4. Higginbotham coined the term "respectability politics" to refer to the ways that Black women working within the sphere of the Baptist Church in the late nineteenth and early twentieth centuries countered racial injustice by promoting norms of Black behavior that accorded with white middle-class norms of "respectable" society, thus hoping to gain acceptance of Black people into white society. As such, it outlined one path through which racial uplift—the belief that through hard work and self-help, Black people could gradually gain equity with white people—could be actualized and promoted women's active role in that uplift through their traditional roles as home, health, and moral leaders. As a practitioner of respectability politics, Daly was certainly not one of the "wayward"

Black women that Saidiya Hartman documents and imagines, but I have borrowed from Hartman's method of seeking out an array of sources and paying close attention to the everyday texture of ordinary lives in order to imagine the richness of those lives. See Evelyn Brooks Higginbotham, *Righteous Discontent: The Women's Movement in the Black Baptist Church, 1880–1921* (Cambridge, Mass.: Harvard University Press, 1994); Kevin Kelly Gaines, *Uplifting the Race: Black Leadership, Politics, and Culture in the Twentieth Century* (Chapel Hill: University of North Carolina Press, 1996); Allyson Field, *Uplift Cinema: The Emergence of African American Film and the Possibility of Black Modernity* (Durham, N.C.: Duke University Press, 2015); Saidiya Hartman, *Wayward Lives, Beautiful Experiments: Intimate Histories of Riotous Black Girls, Troublesome Women, and Queer Radicals* (New York: W. W. Norton, 2019).

5. By white supremacy, I refer to the belief that white people are superior to people of color, a belief that was dominant in the United States in the early twentieth century, and in various forms, remains so today. See Laura Pulido, "Geographies of Race and Ethnicity 1: White Supremacy vs White Privilege in Environmental Racism Research," *Progress in Human Geography* 39, no. 6 (2015): 809–17; Andrea Smith, "Indigeneity, Settler Colonialism, White Supremacy," in *Racial Formation in the Twenty-First Century*, ed. Daniel Martinez, HoSang, Oneka LaBennett, and Laura Pulido (Berkeley: University of California Press, 2012), 55–72; Hartman, *Wayward Lives, Beautiful Experiments*; Bobby M. Wilson, *America's Johannesburg: Industrialization and Racial Transformation in Birmingham* (Lanham, Md.: Rowman & Littlefield, 2000).

6. Cedric J. Robinson, *Black Marxism: The Making of the Black Radical Tradition* (Chapel Hill: University of North Carolina Press, 2000); Laura Pulido, "Flint, Environmental Racism, and Racial Capitalism," *Capitalism Nature Socialism* 27, no. 3 (2016): 1–16; Jodi Melamed, "Racial Capitalism," *Critical Ethnic Studies* 1, no. 1 (2015): 76–85.

7. Melamed, "Racial Capitalism," 77.

8. Janae Davis, Alex A. Moulton, Levi Van Sant, Brian Williams, "Anthropocene, Capitalocene, ... Plantationocene?: A Manifesto for Ecological Justice in an Age of Global Crises," *Geography Compass* 13, no. 5 (2019): 124–38; Clyde Woods, *Development Arrested: The Blues and Plantation Power in the Mississippi Delta* (New York: Verso, 2000); Levi Van Sant, "'Into the Hands of Negroes': Reproducing Plantation Geographies in the South Carolina Lowcountry," *Geoforum* 77 (2016): 196–205; Wendy Wolford, "The Plantationocene: A Lusotropical Contribution to the Theory," *Annals of the American Association of Geographers* 111, no. 6 (2021): 1622–1639.

9. Mark Duffield, "The Liberal Way of Development and the Development-Security Impasse: Exploring the Global Life-Chance Divide," *Security Dialogue* 41, no. 2 (2010): 53–76.

10. See Stephanie M. H. Camp, *Closer to Freedom: Enslaved Women and Everyday Resistance in the Plantation South* (Chapel Hill: University of North Carolina Press, 2004); Monica M. White, *Freedom Farmers: Agricultural Resistance and the Black Freedom Movement* (Chapel Hill: University of North Carolina Press, 2018); Mona Domosh, "Those 'Gorgeous Incongruities': Polite Politics and Public Space on the Streets of Nineteenth-Century New York City," *Annals of the Association of American Geographers* 88, no. 2 (1998): 209–26; James C. Scott, *Weapons of the Weak: Everyday Forms of Peasant Resistance* (New Haven: Yale University Press, 1987); Patricia S.

Mann, *Micro-Politics: Agency in a Postfeminist Era* (Minneapolis: University of Minnesota Press, 1994).

11. Ann Laura Stoler, *Along the Archival Grain: Epistemic Anxieties and Colonial Common Sense* (Princeton, N.J.: Princeton University Press, 2010), 53. For work in historical geography that takes up Stoler's reading of archives as along the grain, see Sarah De Leeuw, "Alice through the Looking Glass: Emotion, Personal Connection, and Reading Colonial Archives along the Grain," *Journal of Historical Geography* 38, no. 3 (2012): 273–81.

12. Stoler, *Along the Archival Grain*, 51.

13. Duffield, "The Liberal Way of Development and the Development-Security Impasse."

14. There are multiple and coterminous histories and geographies of contemporary liberal development practices and ideologies. Scholars from a range of disciplines have documented empirically and theorized extensively the relationships between state-ist improvement projects around the world and the ways in which those projects relied upon and helped to justify racist and often imperial social, economic, and political systems. See, for example, Michael Cowen and Robert W. Shenton, *Doctrines of Development* (New York: Taylor & Francis, 1996); David Ekbladh, *The Great American Mission: Modernization and the Construction of an American World Order* (Princeton, N.J.: Princeton University Press, 2010); Arturo Escobar, *Encountering Development: The Making and Unmaking of the Third World* (Princeton, N.J.: Princeton University Press, 1995); Tania Murray Li, *The Will to Improve: Governmentality, Development, and the Practice of Politics* (Durham, N.C.: Duke University Press, 2007); Katharyne Mitchell, "Education, Race and Empire: A Genealogy of Humanitarian Governance in the United States," *Transactions of the Institute of British Geographers* 42, no. 3 (September 1, 2017): 349–62; Timothy Mitchell, *Rule of Experts: Egypt, Techno-Politics, Modernity* (Berkeley: University of California Press, 2002); Gilbert Rist, *The History of Development: From Western Origins to Global Faith* (London: New York: Zed, 2008); James C. Scott, *Seeing Like a State: How Certain Schemes to Improve the Human Condition Have Failed* (New Haven: Yale University Press, 1998).

15. In 1930, 21,688 acres of Macon County were worked by white tenants, while 104,417 acres were worked by Black tenants. See Charles S. Johnson, *Shadow of the Plantation* (Chicago: University of Chicago Press, 1934), 11. For other accounts of the numbers of white and Black farmworkers in the South, see Natalie Ring, *The Problem South: Region, Empire, and the New Liberal State, 1880–1930* (Athens: University of Georgia Press, 2012); Douglas A. Blackmon, *Slavery by Another Name: The Re-Enslavement of Black Americans from the Civil War to World War II* (New York: Knopf Doubleday, 2008); Pete Daniel, *The Shadow of Slavery: Peonage in the South, 1901–1969* (Champagne-Urbana: University of Illinois Press, 1990).

16. See Sven Beckert, *Empire of Cotton: A Global History* (New York: Knopf Doubleday, 2015); Walter Johnson, *River of Dark Dreams: Slavery and Empire in the Cotton Kingdom* (Cambridge, Mass.: Harvard University Press, 2013); Katherine McKittrick, "On Plantations, Prisons, and a Black Sense of Place," *Social & Cultural Geography* 12, no. 8 (2011): 947–63; Woods, *Development Arrested*.

17. Rosalind Harris and Heather Hyden, "Geographies of Resistance Within the Black Belt South," *Southeastern Geographer* 57, no. 1 (2017): 51–61.

18. For reassessments of Washington's vision, career, and accomplishments at Tuskegee, see Mark D. Hersey, *My Work Is That of Conservation: An Environmental Biography of George Washington Carver* (Athens: University of Georgia Press, 2011); Robert J. Norrell, *Up From History: The Life of Booker T. Washington* (Cambridge, Mass.: Belknap Press of Harvard University Press, 2009). Louis R. Harlan remains the most influential chronicler of Washington's life and accomplishments, see *Booker T. Washington: The Making of a Black Leader, 1856–1901* (New York: Oxford University Press, 1972); and *Booker T. Washington: The Wizard of Tuskegee, 1901–1915* (New York: Oxford University Press, 1986).

19. According to Foucault, biopolitics refers to a form of governance that gains its power through securing a population's purity and safety within the context of an imagined, alien, raced, internal or external threat. In distinction to sovereign forms of power that gain authority through laws and prohibitions, biopower works through various mechanisms—institutions, forms of knowledge, grounded practices—that seek to regulate life at the individual, anatomical level and at the level of populations. The practices of the USDA's cooperative extension service that were aimed at reshaping and "improving" the lives of southern farmers, therefore, were biopolitical in nature. See Michel Foucault, *Security, Territory, Population: Lectures at the College de France, 1977-1978* (New York: Palgrave Macmillan, 2007); Michel Foucault, *"Society Must Be Defended": Lectures at the Collège de France, 1975-1976* (New York: Macmillan, 2003); Mathew Coleman and Kevin Grove, "Biopolitics, Biopower, and the Return of Sovereignty," *Environment and Planning D: Society and Space* 27, no. 3 (2009): 489–507; David Macey, "Rethinking Biopolitics, Race and Power in the Wake of Foucault," *Theory, Culture & Society* 26, no. 6 (Nov. 1, 2009): 186–205; Kevin Grove, "Biopolitics and Adaptation: Governing Socio-Ecological Contingency Through Climate Change and Disaster Studies," *Geography Compass* 8, no. 3 (March 1, 2014): 198–210.

20. Priscilla McCutcheon, "Community Food Security 'for Us, by Us': The Nation of Islam and the Pan African Orthodox Christian Church," *Food and Culture: A Reader*, 2013, 572–86; Priscilla McCutcheon, "Food, Faith, and the Everyday Struggle for Black Urban Community," *Social & Cultural Geography* 16, no. 4 (2015): 385–406; Priscilla McCutcheon, "Fannie Lou Hamer's Freedom Farms and Black Agrarian Geographies," *Antipode* 51, no. 1 (2019): 207–24; Beverley Mullings, "Caliban, Social Reproduction, and Our Future Yet to Come," *Geoforum* 118 (2021): 150–58; Ashanté M. Reese, "'We Will Not Perish; We're Going to Keep Flourishing': Race, Food Access, and Geographies of Self-Reliance," *Antipode* 50, no. 2 (2018): 407–24; Ashanté M. Reese, *Black Food Geographies: Race, Self-Reliance, and Food Access in Washington, DC* (Chapel Hill: University of North Carolina Press, 2019).

21. White, *Freedom Farmers*, 6–8.

22. Adam Bledsoe and Willie Jamaal Wright, "The Anti-Blackness of Global Capital," *Environment and Planning D: Society and Space* 37, no. 1 (2019): 21.

23. Katherine McKittrick and Clyde Woods, "No One Knows the Mysteries at the Bottom of the Ocean," in *Black Geographies and the Politics of Place* (Cambridge, Mass.: South End Press, 2007), 7.

24. Ekbladh, *The Great American Mission*; Matthew Farish, *The Contours of America's Cold War* (Minneapolis: University of Minnesota Press, 2010); Tore Olsson, *Agrarian*

*Crossings: Reformers and the Remaking of the U.S. and Mexican Countryside* (Princeton, N.J.: Princeton University Press, 2017); Christopher Sneddon, *Concrete Revolution: Large Dams, Cold War Geopolitics, and the U.S. Bureau of Reclamation* (Chicago: University of Chicago Press, 2015).

25. Duffield, "The Liberal Way of Development and the Development-Security Impasse," 62.

26. Daniel Immerwahr, *Thinking Small: The United States and the Lure of Community Development* (Cambridge, Mass.: Harvard University Press, 2015).

27. Michael Watts, "Development II: The Privatization of Everything?," *Progress in Human Geography* 18, no. 3 (1994): 371–84; Majid Rahnema and Victoria Bawtree, eds., *The Post-Development Reader*, 1st edition (London: Zed Books, 1997); Richard Peet and Elaine Hardwick, *Theories of Development: Contentions, Arguments, Alternatives* (New York: Guilford Press, 2009); Sneddon, *Concrete Revolution*; Uma Kothari, "From Colonialism to Development: Reflections of Former Colonial Officers," *Commonwealth & Comparative Politics* 44, no. 1 (March 1, 2006): 118–36.

28. Wolford, "The Plantationocene"; Van Sant, "'Into the Hands of Negroes'"; Brian Williams, Levi Van Sant, Alex A. Moulton, Janae Davis, "Race, Land, and Freedom," in *The Sage Handbook of Historical Geography*, eds. Mona Domosh, Michael J. Heffernan, and Charles W. J Withers, vol. 1 (London: Sage Publications, 2020), 178–97; Davis, Moulton, Van Sant, Williams,, "Anthropocene, Capitalocene, . . . Plantationocene?"; Judith A. Carney, "Subsistence in the Plantationocene: Dooryard Gardens, Agrobiodiversity, and the Subaltern Economies of Slavery," *Journal of Peasant Studies* (2020): 1–25; Brian Williams, "'That We May Live': Pesticides, Plantations, and Environmental Racism in the United States South," *Environment and Planning E: Nature and Space* 1, nos. 1–2 (2018): 243–67.

29. Bledsoe and Wright, "The Anti-Blackness of Global Capital."

30. Beckert, *Empire of Cotton*; Andrew Zimmerman, *Alabama in Africa: Booker T. Washington, the German Empire, and the Globalization of the New South* (Princeton, N.J.: Princeton University Press, 2010).

31. Kenneth J. King, "Africa and the Southern States of the U.S.A.: Notes on J. H. Oldham and American Negro Education for Africans," *Journal of African History* 10, no. 4 (1969): 659–77; Kenneth J. King, *Pan-Africanism and Education: A Study of Race and Education in the Southern States of America and East Africa* (London: Oxford University Press, 1971); Patti McGill Peterson, "Colonialism and Education: The Case of the Afro-American," *Comparative Education Review* 15, no. 2 (1971): 146–57; Seppo Sivonen, *White-Collar or Hoe Handle: African Education Under British Colonial Policy 1920–1945* (Helsinki: Suomen Historiallinen Seura, 1995).

32. Stephen Legg, *Prostitution and the Ends of Empire: Scale, Governmentalities, and Interwar India* (Durham, N.C.: Duke University Press, 2014); Cowen and Shenton, *Doctrines of Development*.

33. Sabine Clarke, "A Technocratic Imperial State? The Colonial Office and Scientific Research, 1940–1960," *Twentieth Century British History* 18, no. 4 (January 1, 2007): 453–80; Sabine Clarke, "The Research Council System and the Politics of Medical and Agricultural Research for the British Colonial Empire, 1940–52," *Medical History* 57, no. 3 (2013): 338–58; Helen Tilley, *Africa as a Living Laboratory: Empire, Development, and*

*the Problem of Scientific Knowledge, 1870–1950* (Chicago: University of Chicago Press, 2011).

34. Joanna Lewis, *Empire State-Building: War and Welfare in Kenya, 1925–1952* (Athens, Ohio: Ohio University Press, 2000).

35. Joseph M. Hodge, *Triumph of the Expert: Agrarian Doctrines of Development and the Legacies of British Colonialism* (Athens, Ohio: Ohio University Press, 2007); Joseph M. Hodge, "Science, Development, and Empire: The Colonial Council on Agriculture and Animal Health, 1929–1943," *Journal of Imperial and Commonwealth History* 30, no. 1 (2002): 1–26.

36. King, *Pan-Africanism and Education: A Study of Race and Education in the Southern States of America and East Africa*; King, "Africa and the Southern States of the U.S.A.: Notes on J. H. Oldham and American Negro Education for Africans"; Peterson, "Colonialism and Education"; Sivonen, *White-Collar or Hoe Handle: African Education Under British Colonial Policy 1920–1945*.

37. Timothy Livsey, "Imagining an Imperial Modernity: Universities and the West African Roots of Colonial Development," *Journal of Imperial and Commonwealth History* 44, no. 6 (2016): 952–75.

38. Although the U.S. South was not technically a colonial state nor were African Americans technically a colonized peoples, scholars have pointed out the ways in which the two situations are quite analogous. See for example, Anne-Emanuelle Birn, *Marriage of Convenience: Rockefeller International Health and Revolutionary Mexico* (Rochester, N.Y.: University of Rochester Press, 2006); David R Jansson, "Internal Orientalism in America: WJ Cash's The Mind of the South and the Spatial Construction of American National Identity," *Political Geography* 22, no. 3 (2003): 293–316; David Jansson, "Racialization and 'Southern' Identities of Resistance: A Psychogeography of Internal Orientalism in the U.S.," *Annals of the Association of American Geographers* 100 (2010): 202–21; Jamie Winders, "Imperfectly Imperial: Northern Travel Writers in the Postbellum U.S. South, 1865–1880," *Annals of the Association of American Geographers* 95, no. 2 (2005): 391–410.

39. Sharlene Mollett and Caroline Faria, "The Spatialities of Intersectional Thinking: Fashioning Feminist Geographic Futures," *Gender, Place & Culture* 25, no. 4 (2018): 566. See Kimberle Crenshaw, "Demarginalizing the Intersection of Race and Sex: A Black Feminist Critique of Antidiscrimination Doctrine, Feminist Theory and Antiracist Politics," *University of Chicago Legal Forum* 1989, issue 1, article 8; Kimberle Crenshaw, "Mapping the Margins: Intersectionality, Identity Politics, and Violence against Women of Color," *Stanford Law Review* 43 (1990): 1241–1299; Combahee River Collective, "A Black Feminist Statement," in *The Second Wave: A Reader in Feminist Theory*, ed. Linda Nicholson (New York: Routledge, 1997), 63–70; Mikki Kendall, *Hood Feminism: Notes from the Women That a Movement Forgot* (New York: Penguin, 2021).

40. McKittrick, "On Plantations, Prisons, and a Black Sense of Place," 949.

41. McKittrick, "On Plantations, Prisons, and a Black Sense of Place," 948. For other works that introduce the field of Black geographies see Adam Bledsoe, Latoya E. Eaves, and Brian Williams, "Introduction: Black Geographies in and of the United States South," *Southeastern Geographer* 57, no. 1 (2017): 6–11; Camilla Hawthorne, "Black Mat-

ters Are Spatial Matters: Black Geographies for the Twenty-First Century," *Geography Compass*, July 2019, https://doi.org/10.1111/gec3.12468; Katherine McKittrick, *Demonic Grounds: Black Women and the Cartographies of Struggle* (Minneapolis: University of Minnesota Press, 2006); Katherine McKittrick and Clyde Adrian Woods, eds., *Black Geographies and the Politics of Place* (Toronto: Between the Lines, 2007).

42. Roy Vernon Scott, *The Reluctant Farmer: The Rise of Agricultural Extension to 1914* (Urbana: University of Illinois Press, 1970).

43. B. D. Mayberry, *A Century of Agriculture in the 1890 Land-Grant Institutions and Tuskegee University 1890–1999* (New York: Vantage, 1991).

44. Scott, *The Reluctant Farmer*; R. Grant Seals, "The Formation of Agricultural and Rural Development Policy with Emphasis on African-Americans: II. The Hatch George and Smith-Lever Acts," *Agricultural History* 65 (1991): 12–34.

45. Grace Frysinger, *Home Demonstration Work*, Miscellaneous Publication No. 178 (Washington, D.C.: US Department of Agriculture, 1933); Scott, *The Reluctant Farmer*; Seals, "The Formation of Agricultural and Rural Development Policy with Emphasis on African-Americans"; Carmen Harris, "'The Extension Service Is Not an Integration Agency': The Idea of Race in the Cooperative Extension Service," *Agricultural History* 82 (2008): 193–219.

46. Ring, *The Problem South*; Scott, *The Reluctant Farmer*; Claire Strom, *Making Catfish Bait Out of Government Boys: The Fight Against Cattle Ticks and the Transformation of the Yeoman South* (Athens: University of Georgia Press, 2010).

47. James C. Giesen, *Boll Weevil Blues: Cotton, Myth, and Power in the American South* (Chicago: University of Chicago Press, 2012).

48. William W. Winn, *The Triumph of the Ecunnau-Nuxulgee: Land Speculators, George M. Troup, State Rights, and the Removal of the Creek Indians from Georgia and Alabama* (Macon, Ga.: Mercer University Press, 2015); Kevin Kokomoor, *Of One Mind and of One Government: The Rise and Fall of the Creek Nation in the Early Republic* (Lincoln: University of Nebraska Press, 2019); Angela Pulley Hudson, *Creek Paths and Federal Roads: Indians, Settlers, and Slaves and the Making of the American South* (Chapel Hill: The University of North Carolina Press, 2010); Edward Baptist, *The Half Has Never Been Told: Slavery and the Making of American Capitalism* (New York: Basic Books, 2014); Johnson, *River of Dark Dreams*.

49. Woods, *Development Arrested*, 104.

50. Lee J. Alston and Kyle D. Kauffman, "Up, Down, and Off the Agricultural Ladder: New Evidence and Implications of Agricultural Mobility for Blacks in the Postbellum South," *Agricultural History* 72, no. 2 (April 1, 1998): 263–79; Martin A. Garrett and Zhenhui Xu, "The Efficiency of Sharecropping: Evidence from the Postbellum South," *Southern Economic Journal* 69, no. 3 (January 1, 2003): 578–95; Jonathan M. Wiener, *Social Origins of the New South, Alabama, 1860–1885* (Baton Rouge: Louisana State University Press, 1978); Jonathan M. Wiener, "Class Structure and Economic Development in the American South, 1865–1955," *American Historical Review* 84, no. 4 (October 1, 1979): 970–92; Harold D. Woodman, "Sequel to Slavery: The New History Views the Postbellum South," *Journal of Southern History* 43, no. 4 (November 1, 1977): 523–54; Wilson, *America's Johannesburg*, 75.

51. Daniel, *The Shadow of Slavery*; Blackmon, *Slavery by Another Name*.

52. Wiener, *Social Origins of the New South, Alabama, 1860–1885*; Wiener, "Class Structure and Economic Development in the American South, 1865–1955."

53. Leon F. Litwack, *Trouble in Mind: Black Southerners in the Age of Jim Crow* (New York: Knopf Doubleday, 1998); C. Vann Woodward, *The Strange Career of Jim Crow* (New York: Oxford University Press, 2001).

54. Quoted in Thomas Campbell, "The Saturday Service League" (Auburn: Alabama Polytechnic Institute Extension Service, March 1920), 34.

55. Monroe N. Work, ed., *Negro Year Book: An Encyclopedia of the Negro*, vol. 5 (Tuskegee, Ala.: Negro Year Book Publishing, 1919), 15.

56. Ibid.

57. Maureen A. Flanagan, *America Reformed: Progressives and Progressivisms, 1890s–1920s* (New York: Oxford University Press, 2007); Richard Hofstadter, *The Age of Reform: From Bryan to FDR*, vol. 95 (New York: Vintage, 1955); Corrine M. McConnaughy, *The Woman Suffrage Movement in America: A Reassessment* (Cambridge, UK: Cambridge University Press, 2013).

58. Daniel, *The Shadow of Slavery*; Giesen, *Boll Weevil Blues*; Woods, *Development Arrested*.

59. Isabel Wilkerson, *The Warmth of Other Suns: The Epic Story of America's Great Migration* (New York: Vintage Books, 2010).

60. *United States Department of Agriculture Yearbook 1920* (Washington, D.C.: Government Printing office, 1921).

61. Thomas Campbell, *The Movable School Goes to the Negro Farmer* (Tuskegee, Ala.: Tuskegee Institute Press, 1936); Allen W. Jones, "Thomas M. Campbell: Black Agricultural Leader of the New South," *Agricultural History* 53, no. 1 (1979): 42–59.

62. Sarah Haley, "'Like I Was a Man': Chain Gangs, Gender, and the Domestic Carceral Sphere in Jim Crow Georgia," *Signs* 39, no. 1 (2013): 53–77.

63. Mullings, "Caliban, Social Reproduction and Our Future Yet to Come."

64. Blackmon, *Slavery by Another Name*; Daniel, *The Shadow of Slavery*.

65. Field, *Uplift Cinema*.

66. Robert Pasquill, *Planting Hope on Worn-Out Land: The History of the Tuskegee Land Utilization Project* (Montgomery, Ala.: NewSouth Books, 2008).

67. Pasquill, *Planting Hope on Worn-Out Land*; Robert E. Zabawa and Sarah T. Warren, "From Company to Community: Agricultural Community Development in Macon County, Alabama, 1881 to the New Deal," *Agricultural History* 72, no. 2 (1998): 459–86.

68. Walter Schutz, "Letter from Walter Schutz to Jackson Davis, March 1, 1945," 1945, General Education Board (GEB), series 1, subseries 2, box 287, folder 2991, Rockefeller Archive Center.

### CHAPTER 2. Home Demonstration Work and the Sustaining of Black Life

1. L. C. Hanna, "Supplement to the Annual Report of the Agricultural Extension Work among Negroes in Alabama for the Year Ending December 31, 1929," 13.

2. Sarah Haley, "'Like I Was a Man': Chain Gangs, Gender, and the Domestic Carceral Sphere in Jim Crow Georgia," *Signs* 39, no. 1 (2013): 55.

3. Gargi Bhattacharyya, *Rethinking Racial Capitalism: Questions of Reproduction and*

*Survival* (Landham, Md.:Rowman & Littlefield, 2018); Beverley Mullings, "Caliban, Social Reproduction and Our Future Yet to Come," *Geoforum* 118 (2021): 150–58.

4. Mullings, "Caliban, Social Reproduction and Our Future Yet to Come," 153.

5. Ibid., 153.

6. Douglas A. Blackmon, *Slavery by Another Name: The Re-Enslavement of Black Americans from the Civil War to World War II* (New York: Knopf Doubleday, 2008).

7. See, for example, Susan Lynn Smith, *Sick and Tired of Being Sick and Tired: Black Women's Health Activism in America, 1890–1950* (Philadelphia: University of Pennsylvania Press, 1995); Priscilla McCutcheon, "Fannie Lou Hamer's Freedom Farms and Black Agrarian Geographies," *Antipode* 51, no. 1 (2019): 207–24; Haley, "'Like I Was a Man'"; Tera W. Hunter, *To 'Joy My Freedom: Southern Black Women's Lives and Labors After the Civil War* (Cambridge, Mass.: Harvard University Press, 1997); Nikki Brown, *Private Politics and Public Voices: Black Women's Activism from World War I to the New Deal* (Bloomington: Indiana University Press, 2006); Mullings, "Caliban, Social Reproduction and Our Future Yet to Come."

8. Lisa Emmerich, "'Right in the Midst of My Own People': Native American Women and the Field Matron Program," *American Indian Quarterly* 15 (1991): 201–16.

9. Helen Bannan, "'True Womanhood on the Reservation': Field Matrons in the United States Indian Service" (Sirow working paper no. 19, University of Arizona Press, 1984).

10. Elizabeth A. Gagen, "Making America Flesh: Physicality and Nationhood in Early Twentieth-Century Physical Education Reform," *Cultural Geographies* 11, no. 4 (October 1, 2004): 417–42; Elizabeth A. Gagen, "An Example to Us All: Child Development and Identity Construction in Early 20th-Century Playgrounds," *Environment and Planning A* 32, no. 4 (2000): 599–616.

11. Megan J. Elias, *Stir It Up: Home Economics in American Culture* (Philadelphia: University of Pennsylvania Press, 2008); Carolyn Goldstein, *Creating Consumers: Home Economics in Twentieth Century America* (Chapel Hill: University of North Carolina Press, 2012); Sarah Stage and Virginia Bramble Vincenti, eds., *Rethinking Home Economics: Women and the History of a Profession* (Ithaca, N.Y.: Cornell University Press, 1997).

12. Goldstein, *Creating Consumers*.

13. Grace Frysinger, *Home Demonstration Work*, Miscellaneous Publication No. 178 (Washington, D.C.: U.S. Department of Agriculture, 1933); Roy Vernon Scott, *The Reluctant Farmer: The Rise of Agricultural Extension to 1914* (Urbana: University of Illinois Press, 1970).

14. Frysinger, *Home Demonstration Work*.

15. Goldstein, *Creating Consumers*, 3.

16. Frysinger, *Home Demonstration Work*, 2.

17. Lynne Rieff, "'Go Ahead and Do All You Can': Southern Progressives and Alabama Home Demonstration Clubs, 1914–1940," in *Hidden Histories of Women in the New South*, ed. Virginia Bernhard, Betty Brandon, Elizabeth Fox-Genovese, Theda Perdue, Elizabeth H. Turner (Columbia: University of Missouri Press, 1994), 134–49; Melissa Walker, *All We Knew Was to Farm: Rural Women in the Upcountry South, 1919–1941* (Baltimore: Johns Hopkins University Press, 2000); Melissa Walker, "Home Extension Work among African American Farm Women in East Tennessee, 1920–1939," *Agricultural History*, 1996, 487–502.

18. Bobby M. Wilson, "Race in Commodity Exchange and Consumption: Separate But Equal," *Annals of the Association of American Geographers* 95, no. 3 (2005): 587–606; Bobby M. Wilson, "Capital's Need to Sell and Black Economic Development," *Urban Geography* 33, no. 7 (2012): 961–78; Grace Elizabeth Hale, *Making Whiteness: The Culture of Segregation in the South, 1890–1940* (New York: Knopf Doubleday, 1998).

19. Wilson, "Race in Commodity Exchange and Consumption," 592.

20. Ibid., 599.

21. Wilson relates the case of a Mississippi landlord-merchant who had "boasted that the combination of renting his land and furnishing renters supplies from his store resulted in paying him more than double what it did when he worked 50 slaves on his land." See Wilson, "Capital's Need to Sell and Black Economic Development," 964.

22. For a related study that focuses on Black home demonstration work in Tennessee, see Walker, "Home Extension Work among African American Farm Women in East Tennessee, 1920–1939." Walker's conclusions, that Black home demonstrators were active agents in shaping their work often against what state and federal officials mandated, resonate with my findings in Alabama, Mississippi, and Arkansas.

23. Carmen Harris, "'The Extension Service Is Not an Integration Agency': The Idea of Race in the Cooperative Extension Service," *Agricultural History* 82 (2008): 193–219; R. Grant Seals, "The Formation of Agricultural and Rural Development Policy with Emphasis on African-Americans: II. The Hatch George and Smith-Lever Acts," *Agricultural History* 65 (1991): 12–34.

24. Madge J. Reese, "Report of Girls' Club and Home Demonstration Work in Alabama, December 1914–December 1915," ACES Collection, box 107, Special Collections and Archives, Auburn University Libraries.

25. This analysis is based on the microfilmed state extension reports for Alabama, Mississippi, and Arkansas for the years 1914–1934 that are held at the National Archives, College Park, Md., RG 33, and the reports found at the archive collections at Mississippi State University, University of Arkansas, Auburn University, and Tuskegee University.

26. Mary Feminear, "Report of Home Demonstration Work in Alabama in 1919" (Auburn: Extension Service of the Alabama Polytechnic Institute, March 1920), 40–41; ACES Collection, box 107, Special Collections and Archives, Auburn University Libraries.

27. Victoria Hill, "Cleaning and Laundering Clothes" (March 1920), Cooperative Extension Service Records, box 5, Special Collections, Mississippi State University Libraries; Victoria Hill, "Improvement of the Interiors of Our Homes" (June 1920), Cooperative Extension Service Records, box 5, Special Collections, Mississippi State University Libraries.

28. Anne Jordan, "Living Room Campaign" (Starkville, Miss., 1930), Cooperative Extension Service Records, box 5, Special Collections, Mississippi State University Libraries.

29. Mary F. Killebrew, "Home Demonstration Work in the Black Belt of Alabama" (1921), ACES Collection, box 107, Special Collections and Archives, Auburn University Libraries.

30. May Cresswell, "Home Demonstration Work in Mississippi, 1914–1944" (Starkville, Miss., 1944), Cooperative Extension Service Records, box 5, Special Collections, Mississippi State University Libraries.

31. N. Juanita Coleman, "Annual Report of Home Demonstration Work for Women and Girls," 1919, RG 33, microfilm 4 for Alabama, National Archives, College Park, Md.

32. "A Supplement to the Annual Report on Agricultural Extension Service among Negroes in Alabama (Women and Girls) Movable Schools of Agriculture for the Year Ending December 31, 1921," ACES Collection, box 109, Special Collections and Archives, Auburn University Libraries.

33. Harry Simms and Juanita Coleman, *Movable Schools of Agriculture among Negroes in Alabama*, Circular 39 (Auburn: Alabama Polytechnic Institute Extension Service, 1920), 27.

34. Ibid.

35. L. C. Hanna, "Annual Report for Negro Women, State of Alabama, Year Ending Dec. 31, 1928" (1928), ACES Collection, box 356, Special Collections and Archives, Auburn University Libraries.

36. Gagen, "An Example to Us All"; Gagen, "Making America Flesh."

37. "A Supplement to the Annual Report of the Agricultural Extension Service, Boys Club Work for the Year Ending Dec. 31, 1920" (1920), RG 33, National Archives, College Park, Md.

38. Hanna, "Annual Report for Negro Women, State of Alabama, Year Ending Dec. 31, 1928."

39. Based on research both at Auburn and Tuskegee Universities, I believe these photographs were taken by E. H. Green, a photographer who worked for the USDA in the late 1920s documenting the work of its extension service. Other photographs from this series appear in the photo collection of Auburn University Archives, ACES Collection, RG 71, box 25, with the USDA stamp clearly marked on them, and one of those photos identifies E. H. Green as the photographer.

40. Although the photographs do not identify her as Laura Daly, I've been able to do so by comparing these photos to one from the same series (though not included in the annual report) where she is facing the camera and comparing these to other photos from a later period that identify her by name.

41. Recent scholarship has made clear the importance of cotton production to American capitalism and the making of an American economic empire, see Sven Beckert, *Empire of Cotton: A Global History* (New York: Knopf Doubleday, 2015); Sven Beckert, "From Tuskegee to Togo: The Problem of Freedom in the Empire of Cotton," *Journal of American History* 92, no. 2 (September 1, 2005): 498–526; Edward Baptist, *The Half Has Never Been Told: Slavery and the Making of American Capitalism* (New York: Basic Books, 2014); Walter Johnson, *River of Dark Dreams: Slavery and Empire in the Cotton Kingdom* (Cambridge, Mass.: Harvard University Press, 2013).

42. Hale, *Making Whiteness;* Smith, *Sick and Tired of Being Sick and Tired;* George Yancy, *Black Bodies, White Gazes: The Continuing Significance of Race* (Landham, Md.: Rowman & Littlefield Publishers, 2008).

43. For an excellent discussion of the limitations of those improvements in terms of unequal medical treatment for African Americans, and the implications of those limitations, see Bruce Bellingham and Mary Pugh Mathis, "Race, Citizenship, and the Bio-Politics of the Maternalist Welfare State: 'Traditional' Midwifery in the American South

under the Sheppard-Towner Act, 1921–29," *Social Politics: International Studies in Gender, State & Society* 1, no. 2 (1994): 157–89.

44. R. S. Wilson to Bradford Knapp, "Letter Reporting on Work among the Negroes in Mississippi for the Year 1915," February 12, 1916, RG 33, National Archives, College Park, Md.

45. Ibid.

46. Ibid.

47. R. S. Wilson to Bradford Knapp, "Letter Reporting on Work among the Negroes for the Year 1916," February 19, 1917, RG 33, National Archives, College Park, Md.

48. Louis M. Kyriakoudes, "Southern Black Rural-Urban Migration in the Era of the Great Migration: Nashville and Middle Tennessee, 1890–1930," *Agricultural History*, 1998, 341–51; Louis M. Kyriakoudes, *The Social Origins of the Urban South: Race, Gender, and Migration in Nashville and Middle Tennessee, 1890–1930* (Chapel Hill: University of North Carolina Press, 2003); Joe William Trotter, ed., *The Great Migration in Historical Perspective: New Dimensions of Race, Class, and Gender* (Bloomington: Indiana University Press, 1991); Isabel Wilkerson, *The Warmth of Other Suns: The Epic Story of America's Great Migration* (New York: Random House, 2010).

49. R. S. Wilson, "Annual Report of the Extension Service for the State of Mississippi, 1924," RG 33, microfilm 13 for Mississippi, National Archives, College Park, Md.

50. Ibid., 64.

51. Wilson, "Annual Report of the Extension Service for the State of Mississippi."

52. W. B. Mercier, *Extension Work among Negroes 1920*, U. S. Department of Agriculture Circular 190 (Washington, D.C.: United States Department of Agriculture, 1920), 5.

53. O. B. Martin, *A Decade of Negro Extension Work 1914–1924*, Miscellaneous Circular 72 (Washington, D.C.: U.S. Department of Agriculture, 1926), 1.

54. Ibid., 24–25.

55. Jacqueline M. Moore, *Booker T. Washington, W. E. B. Du Bois, and the Struggle for Racial Uplift* (Lanham, Md.: Rowman & Littlefield, 2003).

56. Julia Pegram, "Annual Report of County Extension Workers, Tunica County, Mississippi, 1923," RG 33, microfilm 13 for Mississippi, National Archives, College Park, Md.

57. "Newspaper Clippings Pertaining to Annual Negro Conference in Regard to Migration North," (Tuskegee, Ala., 1917), Tuskegee University Archives.

58. Thomas Campbell, "Recognition of Negro Progress in the South, Reprinted from the *Montgomery Advertiser*, May 16, 1923," Tuskegee University Archives.

59. Carver was also an early and influential advocate of environmental conservation. See Mark Hersey, "Hints and Suggestions to Farmers: George Washington Carver and Rural Conservation in the South," *Environmental History* 11, no. 2 (April 1, 2006): 239–68; Mark D. Hersey, *My Work Is That of Conservation: An Environmental Biography of George Washington Carver* (Athens: University of Georgia Press, 2011); Monica M. White, *Freedom Farmers: Agricultural Resistance and the Black Freedom Movement* (Chapel Hill: University of North Carolina Press, 2018).

60. George Washington Carver, "Three Delicious Meals Everyday for the Farmer," *Negro Farmer and Messenger*, February 10, 1917, Tuskegee University Archives.

61. Ibid.

62. Thomas Campbell, "Succinct Report on Negro Extension Work for the Year Ending Dec. 31, 1923," Campbell Collection, box 3, Tuskegee University Archives.

63. Ibid.

64. For work that explores the ways in which social reproduction produced value that could not be appropriated by the plantation economy, thereby enabling forms of freedom for enslaved peoples, see Bhattacharyya, *Rethinking Racial Capitalism*; Mullings, "Caliban, Social Reproduction and Our Future yet to Come."

65. Mullings, "Caliban, Social Reproduction and Our Future Yet to Come," 154.

66. Quoted in Hanna, "Supplement to the Annual Report of the Agricultural Extension Work among Negroes in Alabama for the Year Ending Dec. 31, 1929," 19.

67. For discussions of the ways in which colonial archives are structured and the possibilities of finding traces of resistance see Ruth Craggs, "Historical and Archival Research," in *Key Methods in Geography*, ed. Nicholas Clifford, Meghan Cope, Thomas Gillespie, and Shaun French (Thousand Oaks, Calif.: Sage Publications, 2016), 111–28; Sarah De Leeuw, "Alice through the Looking Glass: Emotion, Personal Connection, and Reading Colonial Archives along the Grain," *Journal of Historical Geography* 38, no. 3 (2012): 273–81; Ann Laura Stoler, *Along the Archival Grain: Epistemic Anxieties and Colonial Common Sense* (Princeton, N.J.: Princeton University Press, 2010).

68. Here I am drawing on the work of Lakshmi Padmanabhan who argues that the stillness of such photographic images "is the condition of an active holding in abeyance of contradictory forces: the epistemic capture and vulnerability of the colonized, along with the subject's defiance of her subjection." See Lakshmi Padmanabhan, "A Feminist Still: Documentary Form and Untimely Critique in Sheba Chhachhi's Protest Photography," *Camera Obscura* 35, no. 3 (2020): 18.

**CHAPTER 3. The Movable School and the Aesthetics of Uplift**

1. Beatrice Blackwood, "Diary of Beatrice Blackwood," Beatrice Blackwood Papers, box 18, item 2, Pitt Rivers Museum Collections.

2. Kevin Kelly Gaines, *Uplifting the Race: Black Leadership, Politics, and Culture in the Twentieth Century* (Chapel Hill: University of North Carolina Press, 1996); Jacqueline M. Moore, *Booker T. Washington, W. E. B. Du Bois, and the Struggle for Racial Uplift* (Lanham, Md.: Rowman & Littlefield, 2003).

3. Thomas Campbell, *The Movable School Goes to the Negro Farmer* (Tuskegee, Ala.: Tuskegee Institute Press, 1936).

4. Robert E. Zabawa, "Tuskegee Institute Movable School," in Encyclopedia of Alabama, http://encyclopediaofalabama.org/Article/h-1870.

5. The exact date of when two fulltime USDA agents were assigned to the movable school is contested. Campbell in his 1936 book states that it was in 1914; while Harry Simms, another African American USDA agent, wrote in 1923 that the additional woman agent was added in 1918. See Harry Simms, "The Origin of the Movable School of Agriculture and Home Economics, and How It Is Helping the Negro Farmers Keep Pace with the South's Development," in *King's Agricultural Digest*, 1923, 62–67; Campbell, *The Movable School Goes to the Negro Farmer*.

6. W. B. Mercier, *Extension Work among Negroes 1920*, U. S. Department of Agriculture Circular 190 (Washington, D.C.: United States Department of Agriculture, 1920), 18.

7. Ibid.

8. Ibid.

9. Thomas Campbell, "The First Historical Report on Agricultural Extension Work among Negroes in the States of Alabama, Georgia, Florida, Mississippi, Louisiana, Oklahoma, and Texas" (December 31, 1920), RG 33, microfilm 4 for Alabama, National Archives, College Park, Md.

10. Ibid., 31.

11. Harry Simms and Juanita Coleman, *Movable Schools of Agriculture among Negroes in Alabama*, Circular 39 (Auburn: Alabama Polytechnic Institute Extension Service, 1920).

12. Thomas Campbell, "Preface," in *Movable Schools of Agriculture among Negroes in Alabama*, Circular 39 (Auburn: Alabama Polytechnic Institute Extension Service, 1920).

13. L. C. Hanna, "Annual Report of the Movable School for the Year 1925" (1925), RG 33, microfilm 17 for Alabama, National Archives, College Park, Md.

14. Beatrice Blackwood, "A Day With the 'School on Wheels'" (1925), RG 33, microfilm 17 for Alabama, National Archives, College Park, Md.

15. Here I am drawing heavily from the archival research of J. Emmett Winn, who documents why and the ways in which the USDA produced educational and promotional films that promoted the work of its African American extension service. See J. Emmett Winn, *Documenting Racism: African Americans in U.S. Department of Agriculture Documentaries, 1921–1942* (New York: Bloomsbury Academic, 2012).

16. Ibid.

17. According to Campbell, the film and a projector were part of the standard equipment carried by the movable school. See Campbell, *The Movable School Goes to the Negro Farmer*.

18. Allyson Field, *Uplift Cinema: The Emergence of African American Film and the Possibility of Black Modernity* (Durham, N.C.: Duke University Press, 2015).

19. Claire Strom, *Making Catfish Bait Out of Government Boys: The Fight Against Cattle Ticks and the Transformation of the Yeoman South* (Athens: University of Georgia Press, 2010).

20. Roy Vernon Scott, *The Reluctant Farmer: The Rise of Agricultural Extension to 1914* (Urbana: University of Illinois Press, 1970); Monica M. White, *Freedom Farmers: Agricultural Resistance and the Black Freedom Movement* (Chapel Hill: University of North Carolina Press, 2018).

21. Gabriel Rosenberg, *The 4-H Harvest: Sexuality and the State in Rural America* (Philadelphia: University of Pennsylvania Press, 2016).

22. Martha Hodes, *White Women, Black Men: Illicit Sex in the Nineteenth-Century South* (New Haven: Yale University Press, 1999); Ida B. Wells-Barnett, *On Lynchings* (Mineola, N.Y.: Dover Publications, 2014); George Yancy, *Black Bodies, White Gazes: The Continuing Significance of Race* (Landham, Md.: Rowman & Littlefield, 2008).

23. Campbell, *The Movable School Goes to the Negro Farmer*, 76.

24. Ibid., 134.

25. Ibid., 139.

26. Ibid., 142.
27. Ibid., 134.
28. Ibid.
29. Ibid., 136.
30. Ibid., 137.
31. Evelyn Brooks Higginbotham, *Righteous Discontent: The Women's Movement in the Black Baptist Church, 1880–1921* (Cambridge, Mass.: Harvard University Press, 1994).
32. Kenneth Ames, *Death in the Dining Room, and Other Tales of Victorian Culture* (Philadelphia: Temple University Press, 1995).
33. Campbell, *The Movable School Goes to the Negro Farmer*, 145.
34. Ibid., 156.
35. "A Supplement to the Annual Report on Agricultural Extension among Negroes in Alabama (Women and Girls) Movable Schools of Agriculture for the Year Ending December 31, 1921," ACES Collection, box 109, Special Collections and Archives, Auburn University Libraries.
36. "Liberian Writes of Tuskegee Work, Agent of African Government Shows Value of Extension Service among Negroes," *Montgomery Advertiser*, March 19, 1924, Tuskegee Extension Service Collection, box 2, Tuskegee University Archives.
37. Thomas Campbell, "Annual Report of Negro Extension Work Containing Narrative and Statistics for the Southern States, 1925," RG 33, microfilm 17 for Alabama, National Archives, College Park, Md.
38. "Letter from Amelia Njongwana to T. M. Campbell and E. C. Roberts, in Thomas Campbell's Field Trip Report, August 26, 1928," ACES Collection, box 355, Special Collections and Archives, Auburn University Libraries.
39. "Letter from V. Sibusisiwe Makanya to T. M. Campbell and E. C. Roberts, in Thomas Campbell's Field Trip Report, August 26, 1928," ACES Collection, box 355, Special Collections and Archives, Auburn University Libraries.
40. Campbell, *The Movable School Goes to the Negro Farmer*, 146.
41. E. Kushinga Makombe, "Developing Rural Africa: Rural Development Discourse in Colonial Zimbabwe, 1944–1979," in *Developing Africa: Concepts and Practices in Twentieth-Century Colonialism*, ed. Joseph M. Hodge, Gerald Hodl, and Martina Kopf (Manchester, UK: Manchester University Press, 2014), 159.
42. Margaret Wrong, "Letter from Margaret Wrong to Jackson Davis, April 6, 1944," 1944, Conference of British Missionary Societies, box 8, Archives and Special Collections, School of Oriental and African Studies, University of London.
43. Ruth Compton Brouwer, "Books for Africans: Margaret Wrong and the Gendering of African Writing, 1929–1963," *International Journal of African Historical Studies* 31, no. 1 (1998): 53–71.
44. This suggestion appears in the Conference of British Missionary Societies archive, box 8, at the School of Oriental and African Studies, University of London, under the title "List of Books to Be Translated into TWI and Other Vernaculars."
45. See for example Joseph M. Hodge, *Triumph of the Expert: Agrarian Doctrines of Development and the Legacies of British Colonialism* (Athens, Ohio: Ohio University Press, 2007); Joanna Lewis, *Empire State-Building: War and Welfare in Kenya, 1925–1952*

(Athens, Ohio: Ohio University Press, 2000); Frederick Cooper, *Decolonization and African Society: The Labor Question in French and British Africa* (Cambridge, UK: Cambridge University Press, 1996).

46. Blackwood, "Diary of Beatrice Blackwood."

## CHAPTER 4. Prairie Farms and the Struggle for Black Land Ownership

1. F. Jack Hurley, *Marion Post Wolcott: A Photographic Journey* (Albuquerque: University of New Mexico Press, 1989).

2. I am greatly indebted to the work of Robert G. Pasquill Jr., Robert E. Zabawa, and Sarah T. Warren who documented this history in great detail. See Robert Pasquill, *Planting Hope on Worn-Out Land: The History of the Tuskegee Land Utilization Project* (Montgomery, Ala.: NewSouth Books, 2008); Sarah T. Warren and Robert E. Zabawa, "The Origins of the Tuskegee National Forest: Nineteenth-and Twentieth-Century Resettlement and Land Development Programs in the Black Belt Region of Alabama," *Agricultural History* 72, no. 2 (1998): 487–508; Robert E. Zabawa and Sarah T. Warren, "From Company to Community: Agricultural Community Development in Macon County, Alabama, 1881 to the New Deal," *Agricultural History* 72, no. 2 (1998): 459–86.

3. Monica White's recent reframing of Washington's social and economic philosophy highlights his view of agriculture "as a strategy of freedom and liberation" for Black farmers and the importance of home and land ownership as a means of achieving that liberation. Monica M. White, *Freedom Farmers: Agricultural Resistance and the Black Freedom Movement* (Chapel Hill: University of North Carolina Press, 2018), 50.

4. See, for example, Emily Greenwald, *Reconfiguring the Reservation: The Nez Perces, Jicarilla Apaches, and the Dawes Act* (Albuquerque: University of New Mexico Press, 2002); Eric N. Olund, "From Savage Space to Governable Space: The Extension of United States Judicial Sovereignty over Indian Country in the Nineteenth Century," *Cultural Geographies* 9, no. 2 (2002): 129–57; Debra A. Reid and Evan P. Bennett, *Beyond Forty Acres and a Mule: African American Landowning Families since Reconstruction* (Gainesville: University Press of Florida, 2012); Bruce J. Reynolds, *Black Farmers in America, 1865–2000: The Pursuit of Independent Farming and the Role of Cooperatives* (Washington, D.C.: USDA Rural-Business Cooperative Service Report 194, 2003); Anne Bonds and Joshua Inwood, "Beyond White Privilege: Geographies of White Supremacy and Settler Colonialism," *Progress in Human Geography* 40, no. 6 (2016): 715–33; Laura Pulido, "Geographies of Race and Ethnicity III: Settler Colonialism and Nonnative People of Color," *Progress in Human Geography* 42, no. 2 (2018): 309–18.

5. Walter Johnson, *River of Dark Dreams: Slavery and Empire in the Cotton Kingdom* (Cambridge, Mass.: Harvard University Press, 2013), 226.

6. For analyses of the histories and geographies of other Black towns in the United States see Norman L. Crockett, *The Black Towns* (Lawrence: Regents Press of Kansas, 1979); Danielle M. Purifoy and Louise Seamster, "Creative Extraction: Black Towns in White Space," *Environment and Planning D: Society and Space* 39, no. 1 (2021): 47–66; Karla Slocum, *Black Towns, Black Futures: The Enduring Allure of a Black Place in the American West* (Chapel Hill: University of North Carolina Press, 2019); Arthur L. Tolson, "Black Towns of Oklahoma," *Black Scholar* 1, no. 6 (1970): 18–22.

7. Louis R. Harlan, *Booker T. Washington, The Wizard of Tuskegee, 1901–1915* (New York: Oxford University Press, 1986).
8. Ibid., 170.
9. Warren and Zabawa, "The Origins of the Tuskegee National Forest"; Zabawa and Warren, "From Company to Community County."
10. The community was later called Harris Barrett, named for the Hampton official who was treasurer for the Southern Improvement Company.
11. For a comprehensive analysis of Black economic thought and the importance of collectives to that thought, see Jessica Gordon Nembhard, *Collective Courage: A History of African American Cooperative Economic Thought and Practice* (State College: Pennsylvania State University Press, 2014).
12. Zabawa and Warren, "From Company to Community."
13. "Minutes of Subsistence Homesteads Conference," February 9, 1934, RG 96, box 37, National Archives, College Park, Md.
14. Ibid.
15. In her letter, Daly wrote that "the whole situation offers a splendid opportunity for the development of a Subsistence Homesteads project," offering "to make any contribution I can towards its success." Laura R. Daly, "Letter to Mr. F. D. Patterson, June 27, 1934," RG 96, box 39, National Archives, College Park, Md.
16. "Abstract," Tuskegee, Ala., RG 96, box 36, National Archives, College Park, Md.
17. Zabawa and Warren, "From Company to Community Deal."
18. Veida S. Morrow, "Factual Set-Up of Tuskegee, Alabama, Memo from Veida S. Morrow to John B. Beach," October 24, 1935, RG 96, box 36, National Archives, College Park, Md.
19. Taylor Miller, "Memo from Taylor C. Miller to J. H. Wood," RG 96, box 15, National Archives, College Park, Md.
20. Morrow, "Factual Set-Up of Tuskegee, Alabama, Memo from Veida S. Morrow to John B. Beach."
21. Pasquill, *Planting Hope on Worn-Out Land*; Zabawa and Warren, "From Company to Community."
22. Sara M. Gregg, *Managing the Mountains: Land Use Planning, the New Deal, and the Creation of a Federal Landscape in Appalachia* (New Haven: Yale University Press, 2010).
23. Pasquill, *Planting Hope on Worn-Out Land*, 66.
24. R. W. Hudgens, "Letter from R. W. Hudgens to R. G. Tugwell," May 25, 1936, RG 96, box 74, National Archives, College Park, Md.
25. Katharine F. Dietz, June 14, 1937, RG 96, box 15, National Archives, College Park, Md.
26. A lengthy memo from Taylor Miller outlined in detail the nature of the cooperative loan and the plans for its repayment. Taylor Miller, "Memo from Taylor C. Miller to J. H. Wood in Regard to Cooperative Activities for the Prairie Farms Project," RG 96, box 15, National Archives, College Park, Md.
27. Thomas Campbell, "Cooperative Extension Work in Agriculture and Home Economics, Summary of Negro Work in the Southern States, 1936," Tuskegee University Archives.

28. I believe these photographs formed a portion of the documentation that Tuskegee officials used to gain federal support for their project, although I cannot be certain of that since the photographs located at the Tuskegee Archives are not dated nor are there any direct references to them in textual material. However, the photographs are located in boxes that contain material related to the RA, and their subject matter clearly indicate they depict a region that was deemed poor farmland and that showcased families who were potentially about to be resettled. In addition, appended to most of these photographs are captions that begin with "Exhibit xx" thereby suggesting that they were used as part of Tuskegee's presentation material to the RA regarding their plan for the Tuskegee Land Utilization Program.

29. Cecilia A. Moore, "To 'Be of Some Good to Ourselves and Everybody Else': The Mission of the Cardinal Gibbons Institute, 1924–1934," *U.S. Catholic Historian* 16, no. 3 (1998): 65.

30. Hurley, *Marion Post Wolcott*, 46.

31. Stryker wrote to Wolcott in April of 1939, "I have been checking over the good Negro projects, Prairie Farms is in Alabama, not very far from Gee's bend. Talk to Constance about this, and plan to do it later when convenient." Quoted in Nicholas Natanson, *The Black Image in the New Deal: The Politics of FSA Photography* (Knoxville: University of Tennessee Press, 1992), 60.

32. Ibid., 57.

33. This contrasts with white RA communities in Alabama where housing was constructed of superior materials and included indoor plumbing and up-to-date kitchen appliances. See Susan Elizabeth Hunter, "Subsistence Homesteads in Jefferson County: A Successful 'Experiment'?" MA Thesis, University of Alabama at Birmingham, 2012.

34. R. W. Hudgens, "Letter from R. W. Hudgens to Will Alexander," July 15, 1938, RG 96, box 15, National Archives, College Park, Md.

35. J. O. Walker, "Letter from J. O. Walker to E. S. Morgan, April 29, 1939," April 29, 1939, RG 96, box 15, National Archives, College Park, Md.

36. E. S. Morgan, "Letter from E. S. Morgan to Will Alexander," June 28, 1939, RG 96, box 15, National Archives, College Park, Md.

37. Coleman Camp, "Letter from Coleman Camp to Taylor Miller," September 5, 1939, RG 96, box 15, National Archives, College Park, Md.

38. Taylor Miller, "Letter from Taylor Miller to Coleman Camp," December 3, 1940, RG 96, box 15, National Archives, College Park, Md.

39. E. S. Morgan, "Letter to Will W. Alexander," March 9, 1940, RG 96, box 14, National Archives, College Park, Md.; E. S. Morgan, "Letter to C. B. Baldwin," August 20, 1940, RG 96, box 14, National Archives, College Park, Md.

40. Morgan, "Letter to C. B. Baldwin."

41. Taylor Miller, "Letter to Coleman Camp," February 15, 1941, RG 96, box 15, National Archives, College Park, Md.

42. Ibid., July 14, 1941, RG 96, box 15, National Archives, College Park, Md.

43. Taylor Miller, "Memo to Lewis B. Woodson," October 8, 1941, RG 96, box 15, National Archives, College Park, Md.

44. A. B. Powell, "Memo from A. B. Powell to J. H. Wood," December 30, 1940, RG 96, box 16, National Archives, College Park, Md.

45. Taylor Miller, "Letter from Taylor Miller to Coleman Camp," November 15, 1941, RG 96, box 15, National Archives, College Park, Md.
46. Julian Brown, "Letter from Julian Brown to Coleman Camp," January 29, 1942, RG 96, box 16, National Archives, College Park, Md.
47. Taylor Miller, "Letter from Taylor Miller to Coleman Camp," March 17, 1942, RG 96, box 15, National Archives, College Park, Md.
48. Taylor Miller, "Letter from Taylor Miller to C. B. Baldwin," March 28, 1942, RG 96, box 14, National Archives, College Park, Md.
49. Miller, "Memo to Lewis B. Woodson."
50. Taylor Miller, "Letter from Taylor Miller to Gladstone Hodge," March 29, 1943, RG 96, box 15, National Archives, College Park, Md.
51. Ibid.
52. A letter from Baldwin to Morgan makes reference to Morgan's April request for the liquidation of Prairie Farms Cooperative Association. C. B. Baldwin, "Letter from C. B. Baldwin to E. S. Morgan," June 23, 1943, RG 96, box 15, National Archives, College Park, Md. For an analysis of the various attacks on the FSA and its cooperatives, see Paul K. Conkin, *Tomorrow a New World: The New Deal Community Program* (Ithaca, N.Y.: Cornell University Press, 1959).
53. Taylor Miller, "Memo Accompanying Financial Statement of Prairie Farms Cooperative Association," January 13, 1945, RG 96, box 15, National Archives, College Park, Md.
54. See for example Gregg, *Managing the Mountains*; Conkin, *Tomorrow a New World*; Donald Holley, "The Negro in the New Deal Resettlement Program," *Agricultural History* 45, no. 3 (1971): 179–93.
55. "Plans for Subsistence Homesteads" (1935), RG 96, box 36, National Archives, College Park, Md.
56. Morgan, "Letter from E. S. Morgan to Will Alexander," June 28, 1939.
57. Miller, "Letter from Taylor Miller to Gladstone Hodge," March 29, 1943.
58. Hudgens, "Letter from R.W. Hudgens to R.G. Tugwell," May 25, 1936.
59. R. C. Williams, "Letter from R. C. Williams to Will Alexander," April 8, 1939, RG 96, box 73, National Archives, College Park, Md.
60. Coleman Camp, "Progress Report, Prairie Farms Project" (1939), RG 96, box 74, National Archives, College Park, Md.
61. Ibid.
62. See https://maconk12.org/Wolfe/15185-Untitled.html, accessed June 10, 2021.
63. Emory Ross, "Letter from Emory Ross," April 4, 1945, series 2, box 5, Emory Ross Papers, Special Collections, Burke Library, Union Theological Seminary, New York.
64. Thomas M. Campbell, "Report of Field Trips and Other Activities," October 15, 1945, Campbell Collection, box 019.002, Tuskegee University Archives.
65. Scholars have documented how the Agricultural Adjustment Act, an act that attempted to stabilize agricultural commodity prices by providing subsidies for farmers in exchange for them leaving their land fallow, led to the eviction of tenant farmers and sharecroppers. See Donald H. Grubbs, *Cry from the Cotton: The Southern Tenant Farmers' Union and the New Deal* (Fayetteville: University of Arkansas Press, 1971); Waymon R. Hinson and Edward Robinson, "'We Didn't Get Nothing:' The Plight of Black

Farmers," *Journal of African American Studies* 12, no. 3 (2008): 283–302; Ira Katznelson, *Fear Itself: The New Deal and the Origins of Our Time* (New York: Liveright, 2013).

66. Katznelson, *Fear Itself*.

67. Morgan, "Letter from E. S. Morgan to Will Alexander," June 28, 1939.

68. Miller, "Letter from Taylor Miller to Gladstone Hodge," March 29, 1943.

69. Tania Murray Li, *The Will to Improve: Governmentality, Development, and the Practice of Politics* (Durham, N.C.: Duke University Press, 2007).

70. For recent work that interrogates the linkages between the New Deal and U.S.'s postwar overseas interventions—what came to be called "development"—see David Ekbladh, "'Mr. TVA': Grass-Roots Development, David Lillienthal, and the Rise and Fall of the Tennessee Valley Authority," *Diplomatic History* 26 (2002): 335–74; David Ekbladh, *The Great American Mission: Modernization and the Construction of an American World Order* (Princeton, N.J.: Princeton University Press, 2010); Daniel Immerwahr, *Thinking Small: The United States and the Lure of Community Development* (Cambridge, Mass.: Harvard University Press, 2015); Christopher Sneddon, *Concrete Revolution: Large Dams, Cold War Geopolitics, and the U.S. Bureau of Reclamation* (Chicago: University of Chicago Press, 2015).

## CHAPTER 5. Black Extension Work in the U.S. South and Liberal Development Overseas

1. Thomas Campbell, Jackson Davis, Margaret Wrong *Africa Advancing: A Study of Rural Education and Agriculture in West Africa and the Belgian Congo* (New York: Friendship Press, 1945), 5.

2. M. L. Wilson, "Objectives of the Conference," in *Conference Report on the Contribution of Extension Methods and Techniques Toward the Rehabilitation of War-Torn Countries* (Washington, D.C.: United States Department of Agriculture Extension Service and Office of Foreign Agricultural Relations, 1945), 2.

3. Louise Stanley, "Suggested Approaches for Education for Improvement of Homemaking Practices," in Wilson, *Conference Report on the Contribution of Extension Methods and Techniques Toward the Rehabilitation of War-Torn Countries*, 221.

4. Adam Bledsoe and Willie Jamaal Wright, "The Anti-Blackness of Global Capital," *Environment and Planning D: Society and Space* 37, no. 1 (2019): 8–26.

5. Kenneth J. King, "Africa and the Southern States of the U.S.A.: Notes on J. H. Oldham and American Negro Education for Africans," *Journal of African History* 10, no. 4 (1969): 659–77; Patti McGill Peterson, "Colonialism and Education: The Case of the Afro-American," *Comparative Education Review* 15, no. 2 (1971): 146–57; Donald Johnson, "W. E. B. Du Bois, Thomas Jesse Jones, and the Struggle for Social Education, 1900–1930," *Journal of Negro History* 85, no. 3 (2000): 71–95; Jacqueline M. Moore, *Booker T. Washington, W. E. B. Du Bois, and the Struggle for Racial Uplift* (Lanham, Md.: Rowman & Littlefield, 2003); Kenneth J. King, *Pan-Africanism and Education: A Study of Race and Education in the Southern States of America and East Africa* (London: Oxford University Press, 1971).

6. Hampton Institute (now Hampton University) was founded in 1863 as an institution to provide higher education for African Americans. Like Tuskegee, it focused on training African Americans for jobs in education, agriculture, and industry.

7. Charles Weber, "The Influence of the Hampton-Tuskegee Model on the Educational Policies of the Permanent Mandates Commission and British Colonial Policy," *Africana Journal* 16 (1994): 66–84; Johnson, "W. E. B. Du Bois, Thomas Jesse Jones, and the Struggle for Social Education, 1900–1930"; King, *Pan-Africanism and Education*.

8. Eric Anderson and Alfred A. Moss Jr., *Dangerous Donations: Northern Philanthropy and Southern Black Education, 1902–1930* (Columbia: University of Missouri Press, 1999); Edward H. Berman, *The Influence of the Carnegie, Ford, and Rockefeller Foundations on American Foreign Policy: The Ideology of Philanthropy* (Albany, N.Y.: SUNY Press, 1983).

9. Johnson, "W. E. B. Du Bois, Thomas Jesse Jones and the Struggle for Social Education, 1900–1930."

10. Thomas Jesse Jones, *Negro Education: A Study of the Private and Higher Schools for Colored People in the United States*, Department of the Interior, Bureau of Education, Bulletin, 1916 (Washington, D.C.: Government Printing office, 1917), 1.

11. Ibid., 10.

12. Ibid., 3.

13. Ibid., 10.

14. Andrew Zimmerman, *Alabama in Africa: Booker T. Washington, the German Empire, and the Globalization of the New South* (Princeton, N.J.: Princeton University Press, 2010); King, *Pan-Africanism and Education*; King, "Africa and the Southern States of the U.S.A."

15. King, *Pan-Africanism and Education;* Jake Hodder, "Toward a Geography of Black Internationalism: Bayard Rustin, Nonviolence, and the Promise of Africa," *Annals of the American Association of Geographers* 106, no. 6 (2016): 1360–77.

16. For a summary of these surveys, see L. J. Lewis, "Introduction," in *Phelps-Stokes Reports on Education in Africa* (London: Oxford University Press, 1962).

17. Thomas Jesse Jones, *Education in Africa: A Study of the West, South, and Equatorial African Education Commission, under the Auspices of the Phelps-Stokes Fund and Foreign Mission Societies of North America and Europe* (New York: Phelps-Stokes Fund, 1922), 18.

18. Ibid., 19.

19. Ibid., 22.

20. Ibid., 24.

21. Mark Duffield, "The Liberal Way of Development and the Development-Security Impasse: Exploring the Global Life-Chance Divide," *Security Dialogue* 41, no. 2 (2010): 53–76; Mark Duffield, *Development, Security and Unending War* (Cambridge, UK: Polity Press, 2007).

22. Jones, *Education in Africa*, 31.

23. Ibid., 31. As mentioned in chapter 3, Mrs. Wilkie was a missionary who along with her husband had visited Tuskegee in 1921 and seen the movable school in action.

24. "Memorandum, Phelps-Stokes Fund's Approach to African Work," January 9, 1948, Phelps Stokes Collection, box 1, folder 10, Schomburg Center for Research in Black Culture.

25. Ibid., 1.

26. Ibid., 2.

27. Joseph M. Hodge, *Triumph of the Expert: Agrarian Doctrines of Development and the Legacies of British Colonialism* (Athens, Ohio: Ohio University Press, 2007), 131. For a more detailed account of the complex relationships between the education "experts" at the British Colonial Office and the various international and national missionary societies in Africa that actually provided much of the support for education in Africa, see King, *Pan-Africanism and Education*; Seppo Sivonen, *White-Collar or Hoe Handle: African Education Under British Colonial Policy 1920–1945* (Helsinki: Suomen Historiallinen Seura, 1995); Andrew E. Barnes, "'Making Good Wives and Mothers': The African Education Group and Missionary Reactions to the Phelps Stokes Reports," *Studies in World Christianity* 21, no. 1 (2015): 66–85.

28. Thomas Jesse Jones, *Education in East Africa: A Study of East, Central and South Africa by the Second African Educational Commission under the Auspices of the Phelps Stokes Fund, in Cooperation with the International Education Board* (New York: Phelps Stokes Fund, 1925), 7.

29. Ibid., 7.
30. Ibid., 8.
31. Ibid.,
32. Ibid., 23.

33. Emory Ross, "The Role of Christian Missions in Education and Development in Dependent Territories," *Journal of Negro Education* 15, no. 3 (1946): 324.

34. Emory Ross, "Letter from Emory Ross to Jackson Davis, Feb. 3, 1944," 1944, General Education Board (GEB), box 286, Rockefeller Archive Center.

35. Jackson Davis, "Letter from Jackson Davis to Reuben Brigham, March 9, 1944," GEB, box 286, Rockefeller Archive Center.

36. Emory Ross, "Letter from Emory Ross to Thomas Campbell, March 9, 1944," GEB, box 286, Rockefeller Archive Center.

37. Emory Ross, "Letter from Emory Ross to Mrs. R. B. Shipley," March 24, 1944, GEB, box 286, Rockefeller Archive Center.

38. Jackson Davis, "Letter from Jackson Davis to Thomas Jesse Jones, October 12, 1944," GEB, box 287, Rockefeller Archive Center.

39. Jackson Davis, "Letter from Jackson Davis, December 12, 1944," 1944, GEB, box 287, Rockefeller Archive Center.

40. Walter Schutz, "Letter from Walter Schutz to Jackson Davis, March 1, 1945," GEB, box 287, Rockefeller Archive Center.

41. Davis, Campbell, and Wrong, *Africa Advancing*, 12.
42. Ibid., 32.
43. Ibid., 121.
44. Ibid., 205.
45. Ibid., 7.
46. Davis, "Letter from Jackson Davis to Reuben Brigham, March 9, 1944."
47. Hodge, *Triumph of the Expert*.

48. For an incisive study that shows how British concerns for a stable labor force shaped its postwar conservation efforts in Africa, see Roderick P. Neumann, "The Postwar Conservation Boom in British Colonial Africa," *Environmental History* 7, no. 1 (2002): 22–47.

49. Sabine Clarke, "A Technocratic Imperial State? The Colonial Office and Scientific Research, 1940–1960," *Twentieth Century British History* 18, no. 4 (January 1, 2007): 453–80; Sabine Clarke, "The Research Council System and the Politics of Medical and Agricultural Research for the British Colonial Empire, 1940–1952," *Medical History* 57, no. 3 (2013): 338–58; Joanna Lewis, *Empire State-Building: War and Welfare in Kenya, 1925–1952* (Athens, Ohio: Ohio State University Press, 2000).

50. Joseph M. Hodge, "Science, Development, and Empire: The Colonial Council on Agriculture and Animal Health, 1929–1943," *Journal of Imperial and Commonwealth History* 30, no. 1 (2002): 187.

51. Davis, Campbell, and Wrong, *Africa Advancing*, 76.

52. Joseph M. Hodge, Gerald Hödl, and Martina Kopf, eds., *Developing Africa: Concepts and Practices in Twentieth-Century Colonialism* (New York: Oxford University Press, 2016), 10.

53. Davis, Campbell, and Wrong, *Africa Advancing*, 205.

54. Ibid.

55. Ibid., 82.

56. Ibid., 7.

57. On his return to Tuskegee, Campbell writes to Davis mentioning how he returned home via Union Station after leaving Jones and Davis in Washington, D.C. Thomas M. Campbell, "Letter from Thomas M. Campbell to Jackson Davis," April 13, 1945, GEB, box 287, Rockefeller Archive Center.

58. "Light Is Coming to the Dark Continent," *Newspic*, June 1945.

59. Jackson Davis, "Summary Notes of a Meeting with Robert Lester," April 17, 1945, GEB, box 287, Rockefeller Archive Center.

60. Jackson Davis, "Letter from Jackson Davis to P. H. Eason, January 24, 1946," GEB, box 287, Rockefeller Archive Center.

61. Emory Ross, "Letter from Emory Ross to All FMC Member Boards and Agencies," October 18, 1945, GEB, box 287, Rockefeller Archive Center.

62. Wilson, "Objectives of the Conference," 5.

63. Ibid., 4.

64. Edmund Brunner, "Summary of the Conference," in *Conference Report on the Contribution of Extension Methods and Techniques Toward the Rehabilitation of War-Torn Countries* (Washington, D.C.: United States Department of Agriculture Extension Service and Office of Foreign Agricultural Relations, 1945), 233–34.

65. Ibid., 235.

66. M. L. Wilson, "Letter from M. L. Wilson to L. A. Wheeler," September 30, 1942, RG 33, box 30, National Archives, College Park, Md.

67. M. L. Wilson, "Letter from M. L. Wilson to F. A. Anderson," November 7, 1947, RG 33, box 75, National Archives, College Park, Md.

68. William A. Minor, "Address of Welcome," in *Conference Report on Extension Experiences Around the World May 16–20, 1949* (Washington, D.C.: United States Department of Agriculture Extension Service and Office of Foreign Agricultural Relations, 1951), 1.

69. Ibid., 21.

70. Ibid., 88.

71. *Homemaking Around the World*, 2nd edition (Washington, D.C.: Extension Ser-

vice of the United States Department of Agriculture in Cooperation with the Agency for International Development, 1973), 3.

72. *Homemaking Handbook for Village Workers in Many Countries* (Washington, D.C.: Extension Service of the United States Department of Agriculture in Cooperation with the Agency for International Development, 1981), 11.

73. Ibid.

74. Ibid.

75. Laura L. Lovett, *Conceiving the Future: Pronatalism, Reproduction, and the Family in the United States, 1890–1938* (Chapel Hill: University of North Carolina Press, 2009); L. L. Lovett, "'Fitter Families for Future Firesides': Florence Sherbon and Popular Eugenics," *Public Historian* 29, no. 3 (2007): 69–85.

76. Daniel Immerwahr, *Thinking Small: The United States and the Lure of Community Development* (Cambridge, Mass.: Harvard University Press, 2015).

77. Schutz, "Letter from Walter Schutz to Jackson Davis, March 1, 1945."

78. Immerwahr documents the limitations of community development projects in places like India and the Philippines particularly as they failed to support land redistribution schemes. Immerwahr, *Thinking Small*.

79. Clyde Woods, *Development Arrested: The Blues and Plantation Power in the Mississippi Delta* (New York: Verso, 2000); Pete Daniel, *The Shadow of Slavery: Peonage in the South, 1901–1969* (Champagne-Urbana: University of Illinois Press, 1990).

80. Immerwahr, *Thinking Small*, 178.

81. Cedric J. Robinson, *Black Marxism: The Making of the Black Radical Tradition* (Chapel Hill: University of North Carolina Press, 2000); Bledsoe and Wright, "The Anti-Blackness of Global Capital"; Katherine McKittrick, *Demonic Grounds: Black Women and the Cartographies of Struggle* (Minneapolis: University of Minnesota Press, 2006).

**CONCLUSION**

1. Library of Congress, "Laura R. Daly, Field Representative, Consumer Division, Office of Price Administration (OPA)." LOC.gov. https://www.loc.gov/resource/fsa.8b00847/ (accessed January 17, 2022).

2. University of Mississippi Digital Collections, Archives and Special Collections, "Laura R. Daly to 'Dear Sir,' October 11, 1962," Clio.lib.olemiss.edu; http://clio.lib.olemiss.edu/cdm/ref/collection/jm_corr/id/3220 (accessed June 3, 2019).

3. MLK to Laura R. Daly, April 19, 1966. Thekingcenter.org; https://www.thekingcenter.org/archive/letter-mlk-laura-r-daly (accessed December 12, 2015).

4. Beverley Mullings, "Caliban, Social Reproduction and Our Future Yet to Come," *Geoforum* 118 (2021): 154.

5. Lynne Rieff, "'Go Ahead and Do All You Can': Southern Progressives and Alabama Home Demonstration Clubs, 1914–1940," in *Hidden Histories of Women in the New South*, ed. Virginia Bernhard, Betty Brandon, Elizabeth Fox-Genovese, Theda Perdue, Elizabeth H. Turner (Columbia: University of Missouri Press, 1994), 134–49.

6. Katherine McKittrick, "On Plantations, Prisons, and a Black Sense of Place," *Social & Cultural Geography* 12, no. 8 (2011): 947–63.

7. I borrow this term from Daniel Immerwahr, *How to Hide an Empire: A History of the Greater United States* (New York: Farrar, Straus Giroux, 2019).

8. See the essays in Frederick Cooper and Randall Packard, eds., *International Development and the Social Sciences: Essays on the History and Politics of Knowledge* (Berkeley: University of California Press, 1997).

9. Frederick Cooper and Randall Packard, "Introduction," in *International Development and the Social Sciences*, 30.

10. Daniel Immerwahr, *Thinking Small: The United States and the Lure of Community Development* (Cambridge, Mass.: Harvard University Press, 2015).

11. Mullings, "Caliban, Social Reproduction and Our Future Yet to Come"; Gargi Bhattacharyya, *Rethinking Racial Capitalism: Questions of Reproduction and Survival* (Landham, Md.:Rowman & Littlefield, 2018).

12. Katherine McKittrick and Clyde Woods, "No One Knows the Mysteries at the Bottom of the Ocean," in *Black Geographies and the Politics of Place* (Cambridge, Mass.: South End Press, 2007), 5.

13. These quotes are from Neal's book—*Hope for the Wretched* (p. 122)—that he wrote about his life and experiences in development shortly before he died. It is not clear if the title is a reference to Fanon's *Wretched of the Earth* that was published in English in 1963. In the preface, Neal describes the impoverished peoples living in traditional societies as "the wretched people of the earth." See Ernest Neal, *Hope for the Wretched: A Narrative Report of Technical Assistance Experiences* (Washington, D.C.: Agency for International Development, 1972); Satoshi Nakano, "South to South Across the Pacific: Ernest E. Neal and Community Development Efforts in the American South and the Philippines," *Japanese Journal of American Studies* 16 (2005): 181–202.

14. After her work in Washington, D.C., Laura Daly returned to her USDA job in Tuskegee. Neal was employed at Tuskegee from 1948 to 1954. Neal, *Hope for the Wretched*, 17.

15. *Homemaking Handbook for Village Workers in Many Countries* (Washington, D.C.: Extension Service of the United States Department of Agriculture in Cooperation with the Agency for International Development, 1981), 194.

16. I draw inspiration from the work of Saidiya Hartman and Lisa Lowe who have demonstrated the power of attending to the contingencies of the past—to the "gaps, uncertainties, impasses, and elisions" in the historical record—in order to rethink the present and imagine different futures. Lisa Lowe, *The Intimacies of Four Continents* (Durham, N.C.: Duke University Press, 2015), 175; Saidiya Hartman, *Wayward Lives, Beautiful Experiments: Intimate Histories of Riotous Black Girls, Troublesome Women, and Queer Radicals* (New York: W.W. Norton, 2019).

# INDEX

Addams, Jane, 23
aesthetics of uplift, 61, 124. *See also* photography
Africa: missionaries from, 66–68
*Africa Advancing* (Campbell, Davis, and Wrong), 95, 103–9
Africa survey: Campbell, appointment to, 102–3; and colonialism, 105–7; photographs of, 103; predecessors of, 97–101; purpose of, 95–97
Agency for International Development, 112, 113
Agricultural Adjustment Administration, 76, 93
Alexander, Will, 85

Baldwin, William H., Jr., 74
Baldwin Farms, 74–75
"Better Babies," 31, 114–15
"Black Belt": meaning of, 7
Black extension agents: agency of and constrictions on, 12; children, care of, 29–31; food, 40–41; goals, 41–42; health, 29–31; health care, 40–41; home improvements, 31; objectives diverge from USDA, 28, 34, 36–38, 119; and quiet resistance, 5, 7–9; sanitation, 29–31, 40–41; seasonal variation of job, 29; supervised by white agents, 27–28. *See also* home demonstration work (HDW), overview; racial uplift
Blackwood, Beatrice, 44–46, 47, 51–52, 57, 69
boll weevil, 13, 53–54
Bretton Woods Conference, 110
Brigham, Reuben, 102
British Colonial Office (CO), 11–12, 97, 100, 102–3, 105–6, 107, 120–21

Brown, Lilla D., 69–72, 86, 94
Brown, Mrs., 83
Brunner, Edmund, 109–10
Buck, Harry, 66, 67
Bureau of Home Economics, 23, 96
Bureau of Indian Affairs, 22–23

Camp, Coleman, 69–72, 85–88, 90–91, 94
Campbell, Thomas M.: and Africa survey, 95, 102–3, 109; autobiography, 58–59; extension agent, appointment to, 16, 58–59; on Great Migration, 39; on health care, 40; land ownership, goal of, 93; and movable school, 44–46, 47, 48–50, 56–57, 59; and Prairie Farms, planning for, 76–77; and subsistence homesteads, 75
canning, 23, 26, 31, 69.113, 83, 124
Carnegie Corporation, 107
Carver, George Washington, 39, 47
civil rights movement, 117
Coleman, N. Juanita, 28–29, 50
colonial Pan-Africanism, 99
consumerism: Black exclusion from, 24–25, 29, 42; USDA objectives, shift to, 24, 28, 34, 36–38, 119
Contribution of Extension Methods and Techniques Toward the Rehabilitation of War-Torn Countries Conference, 95–97, 109–12
cooperatives, 74–76. *See also* Prairie Farms
Cresswell, May, 28
criminality, racist assumptions of, 69–72, 73
Crowe, O. C., 62

153

# Index

Daly, Laura R.: education, 2–3; on Homestead Subsistence projects, 75; on land and home ownership, 41, 62; and Office of Price Administration, 117; and overseas home demonstration work, 123; and photography, 31; politics of protest, 117; and racial uplift, 3–4, 41–42; reports of, 1, 3
Daniel, Constance, 80–83
Daniel, Victor, 83
Davis, Jackson, 95, 102–3, 105, 107
Deitz, Katharine, 77–79
development: community, 10–11, 115–16, 121–22, 123; historical geographies of, 9–12; international, 96, 120–25; liberal, 5–12, 97, 121. *See also* Africa survey; Contribution of Extension Methods and Techniques Toward the Rehabilitation of War-Torn Countries Conference
Donma, K. W. G., 66
Du Bois, W. E. B., 8
Duggar, John F., 16
Duncan, Luther, 16

education: and community schools, 90; views on, 11–12, 98–101, 103–6
electricity, 41
Ellison, John M., 102
emigrant agent laws, 14
enticement statutes, 14
Extension Experiences Around the World Conference, 111–12
extension service, foreign, 112

Farm Security Administration (FSA): and photography, 69, 80–83. *See also* Prairie Farms
Feminear, Mary, 26
"field matrons," 22–23
fireless cooker, 26, 28–29, 55, 113
Food and Agriculture Organization (FAO), 111, 113
4-H clubs, 13, 56

Gee's Bend, 83, 86
gendered labor, 21, 24, 28–29, 113, 118; and social reproduction, 21–22, 41. *See also* heteropatriarchal norms
General Education Board, 95, 98, 123
Great Migration, 16, 36–40, 52
Green, E. H., 139n39
Greenwood Village, 74

Hampton Institute, 2, 74, 98
Hanna, Luella: on health and sanitation, focus on, 29; home improvement, importance of, 21; and movable school, 47, 50–51; photography, use of, 42
Hardy Plantation, 45, 68
health and sanitation, 26, 29; and moralizing by whites, 35–36, 39; and Prairie Farms, 89–90, 93; public health nurse, 40; and recreation, 56; work force, care for, 34–38
*Helping Negroes to Become Better Farmers and Homemakers* (USDA), 52–57
heteropatriarchal norms, 79, 98–99; and domesticity and femininity, 22–23. *See also* gendered labor
Hodge, Gladstone, 85, 87–88
home demonstration work (HDW), overview: Black HDW, special considerations for, 28–29, 31–34 (*see also* gendered labor); funding for, 1, 13, 23, 26, 34–36, 47; objectives, consumerism, 26, 27, 31–34 (*see also* consumerism); objectives, practical assistance, 28–29, 31–34; objectives, scientific methods, 13, 23–24; postwar globalization of, 96, 120–25 (*see also* Contribution of Extension Methods and Techniques Toward the Rehabilitation of War-Torn Countries Conference); and Progressive-era movements, comparison, 23; volunteer-led interventions, initial, 26; white HDW and consumerism, 25–28, 31–34. *See also* Black extension agents
home economics, 23–25, 26; globalization, 112–15
home improvements, 34–38, 50, 61–65; and Prairie Farms, 69
*Homemaking Around the World* (Extension Service), 112–15
*Homemaking Handbook for Village Workers in Many Countries* (Extension Service), 112–15, 123–25
Hudan, Mrs., 123–25
Hudgens, Robert W., 77, 89–90
Hull House, 23

immigration: and assimilation programs, 23; decrease in, 36
Indian removal, 14
indoor plumbing, 41, 63, 77, 83
infant mortality, 37, 114–15
International Missionary Council, 95, 107

Jamerson, Mrs., 42–43, 123–24
Jarrett family, 31
Jesup, Morris K., 47
Jesup Wagon, 47
Jones, Thomas Jesse, 98–101, 105, 107
Jordan, Anne E., 27

Killebrew, Mary, 27
King, Martin Luther, Jr., 117
Ku Klux Klan, 14
land-grant universities, 13

land ownership: as extension service goal, 55–56; Jeffersonian vision of, 73; and labor force, 37; and racial uplift, 41, 55, 65, 91; as threat to white supremacy, 55–56, 91, 118–19. *See also* Prairie Farms
Lester, Robert, 107
"liberal": use of term, 6
life-work: knowledge, form of, 22; as resistance, 117–18, 124–25

Makanya, V. Sibusisiwe, 67
malnutrition, 39
Martin, Oscar, 37–38
Mercier, W. B., 37, 47
Meredith, James, 117
Miller, Taylor, 76, 85–88
Minor, William A., 111
"model" communities, 73–77. *See also* Prairie Farms
moralizing, 35–36, 39
Morgan, E. S., 85, 89
Moss, Tom, 62, 64–65
Moton, Robert M., 15, 76, 93
movable school: and agriculture, 63; Black focus of, 49; evolution of, 44–45, 47, 59; and home improvements, 59–65; and land ownership, 67; legitimization of, 47–53, 59; as model, 49, 66–68, 100, 113–16; as nonthreatening to white supremacy, 50–53; and recreation, 56; and respectability politics, 64–65
*The Movable School Goes to the Negro Farmer* (Campbell), 47, 57–65, 67–68
movies, 45, 52–57
Muscogee Creek people, 14

Native American reservation system, 73
Neal, Ernest, 123

*Negro Education* (Jones), 98–101
*Negro Year Book*, 15
Njongwana, Amelia, 67

Office of Price Administration, 117
Omen, Mr., 66
Omen, Mrs., 66
outhouses, 44, 54, 60–61

peanuts, 39, 113
Pegram, Julia, 38
Phelps-Stokes Fund, 98–101. *See also* Africa survey
photography, 30–34, 42, 113–15; before and after images, 31, 50, 53–56, 59–65, 69, 79–83, 91
politics of protest, 117
Polk, P. H., 79–80
Prairie Farms: assessment of, 77, 83, 88, 90–91; goals of, 72, 89–91; improvements, 69; layout of, 77, 83, 88; liquidation of, 88, 90, 93; and photography, 69, 80–83; planning for, 76–77; Prairie Farms Cooperative Association, 83–89; predecessors of, 73–76; problems with, 69–72, 83–88, 93; and scientific methods, 85–86, 89; selection of families, 79–80; and uplift, model of, 77–80; and uplift and land ownership, 83, 93; white resettlement, comparison, 83, 88–89, 93; and wider community, 89–91, 93

Quinn, Henry, 87

racial capitalism, 4, 8, 121–22
racial uplift: explanation of, 3–4, 46; and Black self-help, 61–62; and Great Migration, 38–40; and heteropatriarchal norms, 31; and land ownership, 65, 73–77; as nonthreatening to white supremacy, 40–41; as resistance, 5–6, 7–9, 41–42, 117–20, 121–23, 124–25
recreation, 56
Resettlement Administration (RA), 76. *See also* Farm Security Administration (FSA); Prairie Farms
resettlement communities, 123
respectability, 3, 46, 64–65, 74. *See also* racial uplift
Rockefeller Foundation, 95
Rogers, C. Murray, 91
Roosevelt, Franklin D., 111

# Index

Ross, Emory, 102–3, 107
Rural Life Council, 123

sanitation. *See* health and sanitation
Saturday Service League, 15
Schutz, Walter, 103
settlement house movement, 23
sharecropping and tenancy: and Agricultural Adjustment Act, 93; and debt peonage, 14; and goods, purchase of, 25; laws as control of, 14–16; plantation, legacy of, 14; as problems of southern agriculture, 73; racial demographics, 7. *See also* land ownership
Simms, Henry, 50
Simpson, Mary, 62, 63–64
slavery, 22
Smith, Fred, 91
Smith-Lever Act (1914), 1, 13, 23, 26, 47
social reproduction, 21–22; and racial parity, 41. *See also* gendered labor
Southern Christian Leadership Conference, 117
Southern Improvement Company, 74
Stanley, Louise, 96
stereotypes, 52–53, 56–57, 103
Stryker, Roy, 69, 80
submarginal land and people, 76, 79–80
Subsistence Homesteads, 75

Taylor, Hill, 41, 62–63
Truman, Harry S., 111
Tugwell, Rexford, 77
Tuskegee Farm and Improvement Company, 74
Tuskegee Institute: education, views on, 90; on Great Migration, 38–40; land-grant status, 13; and land ownership, uplift, and racial parity, 9, 41, 119; and "model" communities, 74–76
Tuskegee Land Utilization Project, 76
Tuskegee National Forest, 76

UNICEF (United Nation Children's International Emergency Fund), 113
United Nations Monetary and Financial Conference, 110

"uplift aesthetics," 53–57. *See also* racial uplift
U.S. Agency for International Development (USAID), 123
USDA cooperative extension service: funding for (*see* Smith-Lever Act (1914)); Home Demonstration Unit and consumption, 22, 24–25, 27–28; as model internationally (*see* Africa survey; Contribution of Extension Methods and Techniques Toward the Rehabilitation of War-Torn Countries Conference); objectives of, 4, 7, 13, 24, 34–35, 55–56; and segregation, 13, 27–28, 54–55; and white supremacy, 4, 6–7. *See also* Black extension agents; home demonstration work (HDW), overview; movable school; Prairie Farms

violence, 14
Vischer, Hanns, 100

Walker, J. O., 85
Washington, Booker T.: and land ownership, uplift, and racial parity, 8, 9, 41, 46, 72, 73–77; and movable school, 47, 59
Wheeler, Leslie A., 110–11
white terror campaigns, 56
Wickard, Claude, 107
Wilkie, Mr., 66
Wilkie, Mrs., 66, 100
Williams, R. C., 89–90
Wilson, M. L., 95–97, 109–12
Wilson, Robert S., 34–37
Winger, Mr., 66
Winger, Mrs., 66
Wolcott, Marion Post, 69, 80–83
Work, Monroe, 15
World War I, 15, 36
World War II, postwar: and standard of living, raising of, 106–7, 109–12. *See also* Africa survey; Contribution of Extension Methods and Techniques Toward the Rehabilitation of War-Torn Countries Conference
Wrong, Margaret, 67–68, 95

# GEOGRAPHIES OF JUSTICE AND SOCIAL TRANSFORMATION

1. *Social Justice and the City, revised edition*
   BY DAVID HARVEY
2. *Begging as a Path to Progress: Indigenous Women and Children and the Struggle for Ecuador's Urban Spaces*
   BY KATE SWANSON
3. *Making the San Fernando Valley: Rural Landscapes, Urban Development, and White Privilege*
   BY LAURA R. BARRACLOUGH
4. *Company Towns in the Americas: Landscape, Power, and Working-Class Communities*
   EDITED BY OLIVER J. DINIUS AND ANGELA VERGARA
5. *Tremé: Race and Place in a New Orleans Neighborhood*
   BY MICHAEL E. CRUTCHER JR.
6. *Bloomberg's New York: Class and Governance in the Luxury City*
   BY JULIAN BRASH
7. *Roppongi Crossing: The Demise of a Tokyo Nightclub District and the Reshaping of a Global City*
   BY ROMAN ADRIAN CYBRIWSKY
8. *Fitzgerald: Geography of a Revolution*
   BY WILLIAM BUNGE
9. *Accumulating Insecurity: Violence and Dispossession in the Making of Everyday Life*
   EDITED BY SHELLEY FELDMAN, CHARLES GEISLER, AND GAYATRI A. MENON
10. *They Saved the Crops: Labor, Landscape, and the Struggle over Industrial Farming in Bracero-Era California*
    BY DON MITCHELL
11. *Faith Based: Religious Neoliberalism and the Politics of Welfare in the United States*
    BY JASON HACKWORTH
12. *Fields and Streams: Stream Restoration, Neoliberalism, and the Future of Environmental Science*
    BY REBECCA LAVE
13. *Black, White, and Green: Farmers Markets, Race, and the Green Economy*
    BY ALISON HOPE ALKON
14. *Beyond Walls and Cages: Prisons, Borders, and Global Crisis*
    EDITED BY JENNA M. LOYD, MATT MITCHELSON, AND ANDREW BURRIDGE
15. *Silent Violence: Food, Famine, and Peasantry in Northern Nigeria*
    BY MICHAEL J. WATTS
16. *Development, Security, and Aid: Geopolitics and Geoeconomics at the U.S. Agency for International Development*
    BY JAMEY ESSEX
17. *Properties of Violence: Law and Land-Grant Struggle in Northern New Mexico*
    BY DAVID CORREIA
18. *Geographical Diversions: Tibetan Trade, Global Transactions*
    BY TINA HARRIS
19. *The Politics of the Encounter: Urban Theory and Protest under Planetary Urbanization*
    BY ANDY MERRIFIELD
20. *Rethinking the South African Crisis: Nationalism, Populism, Hegemony*
    BY GILLIAN HART
21. *The Empires' Edge: Militarization, Resistance, and Transcending Hegemony in the Pacific*
    BY SASHA DAVIS
22. *Pain, Pride, and Politics: Social Movement Activism and the Sri Lankan Tamil Diaspora in Canada*
    BY AMARNATH AMARASINGAM
23. *Selling the Serengeti: The Cultural Politics of Safari Tourism*
    BY BENJAMIN GARDNER
24. *Territories of Poverty: Rethinking North and South*
    EDITED BY ANANYA ROY AND EMMA SHAW CRANE
25. *Precarious Worlds: Contested Geographies of Social Reproduction*
    EDITED BY KATIE MEEHAN AND KENDRA STRAUSS
26. *Spaces of Danger: Culture and Power in the Everyday*
    EDITED BY HEATHER MERRILL AND LISA M. HOFFMAN
27. *Shadows of a Sunbelt City: The Environment, Racism, and the Knowledge Economy in Austin*
    BY ELIOT M. TRETTER
28. *Beyond the Kale: Urban Agriculture and Social Justice Activism in New York City*
    BY KRISTIN REYNOLDS AND NEVIN COHEN
29. *Calculating Property Relations: Chicago's Wartime Industrial Mobilization, 1940–1950*
    BY ROBERT LEWIS

30. *In the Public's Interest: Evictions, Citizenship, and Inequality in Contemporary Delhi*
BY GAUTAM BHAN

31. *The Carpetbaggers of Kabul and Other American-Afghan Entanglements: Intimate Development, Geopolitics, and the Currency of Gender and Grief*
BY JENNIFER L. FLURI AND RACHEL LEHR

32. *Masculinities and Markets: Raced and Gendered Urban Politics in Milwaukee*
BY BRENDA PARKER

33. *We Want Land to Live: Making Political Space for Food Sovereignty*
BY AMY TRAUGER

34. *The Long War: CENTCOM, Grand Strategy, and Global Security*
BY JOHN MORRISSEY

35. *Development Drowned and Reborn: The Blues and Bourbon Restorations in Post-Katrina New Orleans*
BY CLYDE WOODS, AND EDITED BY JORDAN T. CAMP AND LAURA PULIDO

36. *The Priority of Injustice: Locating Democracy in Critical Theory*
BY CLIVE BARNETT

37. *Spaces of Capital/Spaces of Resistance: Mexico and the Global Political Economy*
BY CHRIS HESKETH

38. *Revolting New York: How 400 Years of Riot, Rebellion, Uprising, and Revolution Shaped a City*
NEIL SMITH AND DON MITCHELL, GENERAL EDITORS; ERIN SIODMAK, JENJOY ROYBAL, MARNIE BRADY, AND BRENDAN O'MALLEY, EDITORS

39. *Relational Poverty Politics: Forms, Struggles, and Possibilities*
EDITED BY VICTORIA LAWSON AND SARAH ELWOOD

40. *Rights in Transit: Public Transportation and the Right to the City in California's East Bay*
BY KAFUI ABLODE ATTOH

41. *Open Borders: In Defense of Free Movement*
EDITED BY REECE JONES

42. *Subaltern Geographies*
EDITED BY TARIQ JAZEEL AND STEPHEN LEGG

43. *Detain and Deport: The Chaotic U.S. Immigration Enforcement Regime*
BY NANCY HIEMSTRA

44. *Global City Futures: Desire and Development in Singapore*
BY NATALIE OSWIN

45. *Public Los Angeles: A Private City's Activist Futures*
BY DON PARSON, EDITED BY ROGER KEIL AND JUDY BRANFMAN

46. *America's Johannesburg: Industrialization and Racial Transformation in Birmingham*
BY BOBBY M. WILSON

47. *Mean Streets: Homelessness, Public Space, and the Limits of Capital*
BY DON MITCHELL

48. *Islands and Oceans: Reimagining Sovereignty and Social Change*
BY SASHA DAVIS

49. *Social Reproduction and the City: Welfare Reform, Child Care, and Resistance in Neoliberal New York*
BY SIMON BLACK

50. *Freedom Is a Place: The Struggle for Sovereignty in Palestine*
BY RON J. SMITH

51. *Loisaida as Urban Laboratory: Puerto Rico Community Activism in New York*
BY TIMO SCHRADER

52. *Transecting Securityscapes: Dispatches from Cambodia, Iraq, and Mozambique*
BY TILL F. PAASCHE AND JAMES D. SIDAWAY

53. *Non-Performing Loans, Non-Performing People: Life and Struggle with Mortgage Debt in Spain*
BY MELISSA GARCÍA-LAMARCA

54. *Disturbing Development in the Jim Crow South*
BY MONA DOMOSH